M000304027

MY BLESSED

BRIDGES

MY BLESSED
BRIDGES

BOBBIE
TROTTER

TATE PUBLISHING
AND ENTERPRISES, LLC

My Blessed Bridges
Copyright © 2012 by Bobbie Trotter. All rights reserved.

No part of this publication may be reproduced, stored in a retrieval system or transmitted in any way by any means, electronic, mechanical, photocopy, recording or otherwise without the prior permission of the author except as provided by USA copyright law.

The opinions expressed by the author are not necessarily those of Tate Publishing, LLC.

Published by Tate Publishing & Enterprises, LLC
127 E. Trade Center Terrace | Mustang, Oklahoma 73064 USA
1.888.361.9473 | www.tatepublishing.com

Tate Publishing is committed to excellence in the publishing industry. The company reflects the philosophy established by the founders, based on Psalm 68:11,
"The Lord gave the word and great was the company of those who published it."

Book design copyright © 2012 by Tate Publishing, LLC. All rights reserved.
Cover design by Shawn Collins
Interior design by Nathan Harmony
Photos by Megan Trotter

Published in the United States of America

ISBN: 978-1-61862-070-5
1. Biography & Autobiography / Personal Memoirs
2. Philosophy / Social
11.11.29

ACKNOWLEDGMENTS

There are so very many "bridges" in my life that I could not begin to thank them all, but I hold them most appreciatively in my heart. I must thank my family, my children, Ross and Megan, for their patience, pride, and understanding, and my husband, Jack, from whom I learned to be a good writer. There are two more. One is a kind and sweet soul, full of love, who will tear your manuscript to shreds in search of one small imperfection. For her time and her meticulous love of the English language, I thank my dear friend and colleague, Marge DeStefano. Finally, I owe a great debt of appreciation to Callie Ferguson, whose warm encouragement and keen eye has made this work something "of which I can be very proud."

TABLE OF CONTENTS

PROLOGUE

What is a bridge? An engineering feat, the manifestation of the mind's conception. What is a bridge? Humanity's longing to be connected to one another. Great structures, yes, but greater still in their purpose.

I have known great bridges of the world. The Verrazano Narrows Bridge is important to me because it connected me to Staten Island and the home of my first college roommate. I treasure the memories of that brief, festive time in which we finally became friends, different as we were. Consequently, I grieved terribly that following summer when she died in an automobile accident in Lake George. I lost her presence and the promise of our future friendship, yet I have forever felt connected to her and her family.

Crossing the bridge brought me into their lives, and they into mine, irrevocably. And I sought solace in the words of the English writer John Donne: "No man is an island entire of itself; every man is a piece of the continent, a part of the main...any man's death diminishes me, because I am involved in mankind... and therefore, never send to know for whom the bell tolls; it tolls for thee."

As an English teacher, I have seen the London Bridge several times and marveled at it. Not only does it connect the city of London but also the world and the world of time. It connects us in time to the dreams, desires, ambitions, loves, hatreds, revenge, fears, foibles, and tragedies of past men and women, very much like us.

As a young, impressionable person, I watched the movie *The Bridge Over the River Kwai* and was irresistibly connected to the human spirit, the ability to sacrifice, endure, love, and even die for one another, for the ideals one believes in, and for freedom. Bridges, in my mind, have since stood for freedom, so very different from walls.

Sydney Harbor Bridge delivered me from the horrors of war. My friends have often teased me that I "flew into Vietnam a hawk, and flew out a dove." I was six months in country, halfway through my tour, when I got my first leave, R&R to Australia. I crossed the great span of bridge, looking at the famous Opera House, still thinking about the dead and wounded friends I left only hours behind, the orphaned children, the ancient destroyed monuments, the polluted water, the corruption and drugs, the stench that was Vietnam in 1971. By the time I crossed the bridge again one week later, I had regained the heart to go back and fulfill my mission, which was now to tell the world that war does not build bridges, or anything. Nobody wins in war. It is in peace and freedom that mankind builds great cities with funny-looking opera houses where voices can ring out the shared song of life.

My husband, at the time, fiancé, informed me most emphatically that he did not wish to wear a wedding ring. Back then, he had a few peculiarities, this man who spent a year at college, never wearing shoes. It was one of many barriers we had to overcome in our lives together. During Easter vacation, as I led my exchange students around the usual tourist sights in Florence, Italy, I was drawn, as if by some unseen power, pointing its finger to the goldsmith shops on the Ponte Vecchio, one of Italy's oldest and most romantic bridges. I found a band that fit my third finger, left hand perfectly. I tried another, larger one on my forefinger, hoping it was just right for his third finger, left hand. I gave it to him one week later, at his parents' house. In thirty-five years, the man has never once removed that gold band. Since then, we have spent the better part of our lives crossing bridges together.

Girl Scouts is a wonderful organization, made especially wonderful because it's a woman's twist on an already wonderful organization, Boy Scouts. Boys move progressively through their ranks as they learn and mature; girls "cross over" in bridging ceremonies to signify their growth, development, and connection to the world. The year that my daughter was ready to cross over into Junior Girl Scouts, our family planned a trip across country. It was the right time, since my brother was stationed at Beale Air Force Base, California. We had a small ceremony for her with her troop in Allentown, Pennsylvania just before the end of the school year. When we left in early July, we packed her old sash and new merit badge sash and the next-sized uniform.

We planned it for months. We coordinated it with long telephone discussions over long distance. The logistics were challenging, but the love and pride made it happen. Mom, Dad, brother, aunts, and uncles were all there to see my daughter crossing over into Junior Girl Scouts *on the Golden Gate Bridge!* It was a momentous occasion that brought not only our family together forever in memory of it but also all the strangers who drove by wondering what those people were doing. My daughter, now looking forward to having little Girl Scouts of her own, often speaks of that wonderful moment. It is a great bond between us that bridges our differences in generation, experience, and thought.

Oh, the bridges! They make our journeys through life possible. They appear in many ways. Sometimes they are great structures carrying us to strange and wonderful places; sometimes they are great changes, events that alter our directions; sometimes they are people who touch our lives; sometimes they are even a still, small voice in the mist that beckons us to abandon our fear, don't look down, and dare to come across.

I am deeply grateful for all the bridges so far in my life. I look forward to crossing so many more until, at last, I can cross that ultimate bridge to the final place of peace and freedom. This work is about those bridges.

DUNCAN, MY DARLING

He was short. By anybody's standards, the guy was short, really short. He had this kind of "boxy" little body, all muscle and sinew, always ready to pounce upon the next moment's excitement. And such a cute butt! I used to just melt as I held back several paces on our walks so that I could watch that butt sway as he walked ahead of me, looking back and with an accusing eye, asking me why in the world I wasn't keeping up. The way a man walks tells a lot about his character. Does he walk tall and proud, no matter his stature? Does he walk as if in control of life or a victim of it? Does he walk as if in the presence of all that surrounds him, aware and calculating? Does he embrace life, or merely roll with it? So much is revealed in the walk. This guy had the stride of one who knew that "the universe was unfolding as it should" (Desiderata 6:7, Max Ehrman), and all was well with him and God. With him, I always felt as if I was learning something about life, that yes, it could be; it is simple. It was as if he was saying, "Anybody can get this. All you have to do is decide, then let it be."

He was hairy too. God gave him way more hair than he needed in modern evolution. No matter though; he could always get a haircut. To know him was to know one of the finest souls to live on God's earth. Such intensity, no matter what the situation. Those dark, blackish-brown eyes would freeze and warm me at the same time, lifting me out of time and space and drawing me into his special soul. He had the amazing ability to take what he had and not only make it work for him but also make it an admirable virtue. Take the beard, for example. This guy toted a thick, black beard that made men envy and women just desperate to brush it, even when he had the occasional piece of food stuck in it! Imagine a guy who could still look dignified with spaghetti or chicken hanging on his face. There was a fire that burned in him that was more contagious than any hallelujah hymn I ever heard in a Baptist revival! *God, I loved that guy!* He brought out the very best in me and everybody else who ever knew him.

He would have been a great father, but that adventure was cut short in his youth. He seemed to commune with all things, both old and young. Old people came alive around him, and children just couldn't get enough of his attention and affection. Women just plain swooned over him, but I never got jealous. I knew without a word ever being spoken that he was mine, all mine, so let the women make fools of themselves! I had nothing to fear.

A true Scot through and through, he was brave to insanity, loyal to death, extravagant with his love, unconquerably dignified, tight with his treasures and stubborn, stubborn, stubborn. I was longing for his kind of love and he found me in my midlife crisis. I was much too old to go so "gaga" over a young man like him, or any man for that matter, but Duncan was no ordinary man. He came from some questionable stock among the Amish of Lancaster County, and if I'd had my senses about me, I might have known there was heartbreak down the road, sooner rather than later. No matter, he showed off his prowess for me, and I couldn't get enough of him. I'd take my chances.

Ours quickly became a relationship that would be hard for most to understand, because it was so free, so open. There were no demands or expectations. There was only, "I'm here. I'm me. Can you accept that? If so, I'm here for you, and there are no limits to that." I'd never known anything quite like this.

My family accepted him immediately. I'm not sure if that had to do with all my previous personal failures or with his inimitable charm. No matter. We almost instantaneously became "a family"; he was one of us, and that meant that we would defend to the death "right or wrong," and we would hold together to the end no matter what outside force tried to intervene. He was part of us.

Why not? It was so easy for everybody to love Duncan. I would get so frustrated, trying to get to places on time. We would come out of the house, and it was as if some kind of radar went off for the kids in the neighborhood. They would just know that we were "out there," and they would come running, demanding Duncan's attention. We would inevitably be late because Duncan would always take time for the kids. In this, as I look back, he was trying to teach me, but I was more concerned with what people would think if we were late, how this would reflect on my future potential in this job, or that organization. I mostly missed the whole point, but he never chastised me. He just continuously made me late.

Nevertheless, I couldn't be angry with him, with those incredible, penetrating, ebony eyes that stopped me cold and forced me to look at myself. I didn't always like what I saw, but I knew with him that he was always more forgiving of me than I was. Duncan never criticized me. He had more subtle ways of teaching me what I needed to know about myself. He made me feel very humble at times. I would look at his beauty, watched how he lived his life, and just know that I was witnessing the work of God.

I adored him. I guess I had forgotten the dream, the expectation, and the hope that love could be like this. All along I knew he was making me a better person. Oh, the good times we had together! Let's talk about the outdoors. Oh my God! How he loved the outdoors. And the things we dared do together! I will never forget the exuberance of a first winter snow as he reveled in it, tossing piles of white stuff into the air in sheer abandon. Then, there were the few Memorial weekends we had at Boy Scout camp, the boys all gone back to school now, when we had the facilities to ourselves, the big house with all the rooms to chase each other through, the great kitchen and all the good cooking, the beach with the wonderful diving off the docks, the row boats and canoes, not to mention the hiking into the fabulous woods! Just us. What glorious days!

He didn't care much for swimming. Maybe it's harder for short guys; they have to work at it, and one criticism, if you could call it that, was that he was not particularly fond of work. Duncan seemed to like the rowboat the best. I had to do the rowing, of course, and he would stand full height, such as it was, face pointed into the wind, beard blowing as if he was a Viking lord. Then, at the end of the day, we would sit, cuddled, watching the crimson sun go down, no matter how long it took or how cold it got. I used to tease him, "What are you, the pharaoh who has to put the sun to bed?" He'd just dance around a little bit on those short legs and laugh his funny little laugh. Bed always seemed like a good idea to him.

I can hardly speak of the regular walks that we took in the Allentown Park system. These were our most treasured moments. The city fathers in their most infinite wisdom, suffering the pressures of the Depression, built this incredibly beautiful system of parks along the Little Lehigh River. It sings the songs of desperation of those who built it, mostly Eastern European immigrants, folks like my own parents who came here filled with hope and faith and a willingness to work to the bone for their dreams. They did this thing! And they gave it to us, so that on any given morning, Duncan and I could walk and meet other walkers: dogs, horses, squirrels, and innumerable birds and insects, yes, and even fish. We could take a few moments out of the crazy lives the world would impose on us to observe and appreciate the greenness of things, the ducks swimming and nesting on the stream, the willows bending into the water, the squirrels and cranes, and bluebirds and cardinals, all enjoying the glory of life as God has given it to all of us.

We explored miles and miles of the system together, through all the seasons, taking in the respective flavors of spring, summer, autumn, and winter. I am forever entranced by the flight of birds, and Duncan would sometimes purposefully startle them, sending them up, just so I could see their amazing grace and beauty. We both ignored their squawking, because we were too busy laughing. Occasionally, I would cry too, in appreciation. He made me do things like that.

Our moments in the park were probably the most deeply meaningful moments I shared with my true love. It was here that we were able to shut out the craziness of the "real world" in which we lived, and the one place where we, together as loving souls, were able to make sense of what our purpose in life on earth must be. I dare say, it was here that on one July morning, cool and crisp before the rush of the day's activities, that Duncan and I stopped briefly—alone, isolated on a hillside, and met "the Holy Ghost." I'm glad Duncan was with me, lest I be able to recognize what we had met in our morning walk. It is hard, if not impossible to tell anyone what it is like to have that moment, let alone to have it together with someone you love. There we stood, as if lifted out of our world, in that simple, ordinary space, suddenly filled with an overwhelming sense of peace and understanding that all was as it should be. No need to worry, there was always an inexhaustible energy of love to tap into.

I was not consciously looking for that, yet there it was, and I was mesmerized until a blue heron flew across the field, and I was once again aware of my surroundings. Duncan merely traced its flight with his keen eyes. I can never pass that particular spot without being taken by surprise and wonder at how the Spirit works. Some would be disappointed for lack of bells and whistles. I was simply, quietly, peacefully astounded. Duncan just sat there, taking it all in with his cavalier, "I keep trying to tell you," attitude, which often ticked me off, but not that morning.

Other times in the park were not so profound, but they sure were special. We had this one place where we always stopped for a moment or two, looked at each other in a knowing way, made our individual absolutions, and moved on. It was a strange, unusual formation in nature where two separate trees had reached for the sun together and became intertwined, their branches wrapped around each other. I told Duncan that these trees got to hug each other every day. No question, these were the hugging trees, the Pryamus and Thisbe, Orpheus and Eurydice, Romeo and Juliet of the forest! And then there was the covered bridge. We always saved the covered bridge for last, as it was close to the parking lot, but also because it was so special. We used to reminisce about how young lovers parked in the old days, under these bridges. What promises, what dreams were made, what comfort those old bridges offered in a storm, especially for a horse!

Oh, but there were so many other good times we shared—wonderful, laughter-filled holidays when he would inevitably overstuff himself and have to sleep it off. There were trips, lots of trips. He loved to travel and was very good about it. We even flew to the Azores and lived together there with my brother for a whole summer. There was this little German girl there who often came to visit, and I thought he kind of fancied her. One day though, we got separated and couldn't find each other. When we did, our joy was so overwhelming that I never doubted again that Duncan lived for me.

He was truly, truly in his element when we went to the Celtic Classic in Bethlehem. I especially remember our first year. He was into everything, as fast as he could go. He loved the pipes and the poles, the lads and the lassies, as well as the games. The border collies herding ducks and geese through little barriers fascinated him. I think he thought that was fine for them, a little silly perhaps, but he admired their willingness to work so hard. His favorite part of the festival was naturally, the food.

This guy's affection was ever present. He'd kiss me any time, any place, and sometimes it was embarrassing and even annoying. I'm glad, however, that I never chastised him for it. He had the sweetest kisses. I know now that you have to give affection *whenever* you can, another thing he taught me. Oh, the best times were when he would just plop down and go spread eagle on the couch or the floor, daring me to attack him with kisses and tickles and belly rubbing. We'd romp and roll and giggle, always ending up in a quiet cuddle.

I really did come to believe that this could last forever, but nothing on this earth seems to last forever. I had found Duncan, or rather, he found me in the spring when everything was fresh and new and full of promise. Only six years later, I was to lose him in the winter, just before Christmas. The cancer came in March. He had these funny little bumps around his throat, which we ignored at first, thinking just a passing cold or minor infection that would take care of itself. One day, his cheeks swelled up like he had ping-pong balls in them. "Enough!" I said, "We're going to the doctor." It wouldn't have mattered anyway. It was lymphoma; no cure, only treatment. Being his stoic self, he was ready, but I was not. We decided to try the treatment, rather I know now it was because we in our grief, our inability to imagine life without him, compelled him to go through this, just to buy a little more time, to try to make a deal with the gods. He knew better, but if it was what I wanted, needed, he'd do anything for me.

These are the times when the sacred meaning of "family" becomes so painfully clear. It wasn't just him and me; we were all of us going through this together, like somehow if we shared the agony, spread it a little thinner, it would be more bearable. We all began to shuffle our busy schedules to accommodate the treatments. We learned a whole new vocabulary, words like *remission, intolerance, cytopenia, vincristine, cyclophosphamide, slow drip, anemia,* and *dose intensity*. We discovered all kinds of drugs for every imaginable purpose, the names becoming part of our daily conversation, in spite of the difficulty in pronouncing them. The initial round of chemo was very aggressive. He seemed to be responding well at first, and then suddenly he became so de-hydrated that he had to be hospitalized and monitored for a week. Even so, in his weakened state, he was the darling of all the staff. "Our special one" they called him. I was not surprised.

In a few weeks, given his remarkable spirit, no one could ever tell he was a cancer patient. I began to believe in miracles. By now, it was summer, and we resumed our walks in the park, only this time, I looked for the Holy Ghost every day. We walked more slowly and looked at a lot more things. We took time to say "hello" to every passerby. We took a great deal of time for one another. Every experience, every sensation was so sharp, so keen, so exquisitely painful. I didn't know he was preparing me because I was still in serious, defiant denial.

It was at this time that we "accidentally" discovered the shrine of the "little priest," Padre Pio off Route 100. We often came home that way on our return from treatments in Philadelphia. I was intrigued, because one of my students had written a paper about Padre Pio. Duncan, of course, acted as if he always knew that the place was there. He loved it and seemed very comfortable and peaceful in that space. In fact, he took every opportunity to mark it as his own.

We stopped many times and lit candles, but I remember one time in particular; it was just between sunset and darkness when we got there. "It's probably closed, "I told Duncan, but he insisted that we stop. There was only one car in the lot, and when the driver saw us drive up the hill toward the shrine, he followed us.

"What is it you want?" he asked. I explained, and he answered, "I'm a postulate for the shrine." He seemed to express such genuine concern for us.

"Sadly," he confessed, "our beloved shrine is known for drug deals after dark. There are those who just do not understand the sacredness of this place. Come, I will stay with you until you finish your prayers."

He gave Duncan a rosary and a vile of holy water from the Vatican. Duncan flashed a quick glare at me, indicating that I need not mention that he wasn't Catholic. In our conversation, though, I was amazed. He claimed to know Duncan's doctor and said that he went to med school with her and even referred to her by her "nickname." He told us much about Duncan's treatment and what to expect; he even seemed to know a lot about Duncan. When we parted, he said he would pray for me. We never saw him again, and Duncan's doctor couldn't quite remember him. Every time the subject came up, Duncan would give me an exasperated look with those big brown eyes. I'd have to shake my head and recite for him, "Yes, yes, angels come in many suits."

Summer faded all too soon, but we both embraced the autumn, our favorite season. He was nuts, of course, over the kids on Halloween, and he pigged out over Thanksgiving. Things started shifting in early December. The drugs just weren't working so well anymore. We tried different drugs. During the long treks up and down the turnpike for treatment, I cried a lot. He just looked at me as if I was stupid, but of course, lovingly. I'd stop crying, laugh at him, and then we'd stop for ice cream. He had a passion for ice cream!

Around the middle of December, nothing could stop the swelling of the lymph nodes all over his body. In bed at night, I would suppress my screams as I lay listening to his labored breathing. My hand across Duncan's chest, I would beg God to take this back and reverted to my old-fashioned Catholic upbringing, wondering what I had done to deserve this. How incredibly egocentric of me! I couldn't see then the blessing God was giving me in sharing Duncan's death this way.

It was all over on a cold, dark, snowless December night, around eight o'clock. It was a dignified death, of course; it could be no other way for him. The whole family was there beside him, each touching him in some way. Even the hospital staff was all crying. But with every gasp for breath, someone had something wonderful to say about my guy. There were stories, lots of rememberings, and we all laughed together right up to the very end, the last breath, and that simple sinking that comes with the surrender. He never closed his eyes. I knew he wouldn't. He always had his gaze set on something the rest of us couldn't quite see. He left us knowing full well that he was much loved and had accomplished his mission. Fearless in life, he embraced death with such a simple pleasure, such an easy slide into the next realm. He lived a life of example.

In my grief, at first, I wanted to be the old Greek wailing women in black who howled over the corpse, beat their chests, and tore out their hair. I understood the sense of this custom. *I wanted to be the one who got to die!* At first, the emptiness was awful, especially when I reached over to his seat in the car, and when I walked in the park, looking for him. When I reached the hugging trees, I wanted to scream until my agony reverberated off all the trees and drifted down into the stream so the waters could carry my pain away. I totally avoided the covered bridge. Instead, I went to work, to teach and to serve in the National Guard, things of which he highly approved and was always willing to wait for. I instinctively knew that is what he wanted me to do; it was all I could do, and I guess it served to heal or help me.

But then, after a little while, I began seeing him again. Oh, not really "seeing" him. It was more like feeling his presence, but that feeling let me visualize him in my mind's eye. It was then that I began to fully understand the essence of his love and knew that he hadn't left me at all, never would. He was much too stubborn for that. It's like he used to do in the king-sized bed on Saturday mornings. He was merely shifting positions. He still waits patiently for me, as he always did, oh stupid, slow learning me.

It's over a year now. I've been through all the variations of the seasons: spring to summer, summer to autumn, autumn to winter. I face another spring in a few weeks, and my heart sings out to me, "It's time, it's time to start again and open more doors to let the fresh air and sunshine in. The business, the purpose of being on earth, is to live life as fully as Duncan did. "There are seedlings waiting to become flowers." He tells me from a distant place that there are others, and they need me, as I need them. He says I must open my heart to them as I did to him. "In an instant they will come through," he says.

Most importantly, I began to understand that things that start on earth, which seem not to last on earth, do not necessarily end. Shakespeare was right. "All the world's a stage…" We move in and out of this place, sometimes separately, sometimes together, all of us ultimately seeking our Maker where and when we can feel as one. For now, whenever I want to, because I was blessed with a good teacher, I can focus my mind and see what I need and want to see; I can take a walk in the park and experience the Holy Ghost; I can hang back a little to admire that proud prance, go gaga over that cute butt, and marvel at the strength and grace in such short legs—all four of them!

THE FAT MAN IN THE RED POLKA-DOT BATHING SUIT

It was the summer after I had memorized the Twenty-third Psalm, "The Lord is my Shepard; I shall not want" (Psalms 23:1, KJV). I was too young to understand the words, but they sounded pretty to my future poet's ear. I was sixteen, too young to die, most people would say. I had everything in the world to look forward to. I was just beginning to show creative promise. My first published poem appeared in the school newspaper. It might as well have been the Pulitzer Prize.

I had no boyfriend yet, and I still liked my mother, though we *did* bicker over almost everything. I loved my younger brother, Mikey, terribly since we were seven years apart and I viewed myself as his second mother, in spite of how pesky he could be at nine years old. He liked to call me Magee, accent on the "gee," after the folksong "Bobby Magee." I was admittedly beaming when he finally took to the water, after all my patient instruction. This was the first summer that I could honestly say he could swim. True, it was only five or six strokes at a time, but he *was* swimming! Now, my older brother, that's another story. The seven years between us may as well have been a hundred. He had no time for me or Mikey except to give us an "Indian rub" on the head or a "rope twist" on our wrists. My mother had appropriately nicknamed him "Butch" when he was little. He seemed to relish in his power over us. He was cruel, and we worshiped him.

All things considered, the prospect of a trip to Florida and back with my mother and two brothers had a certain allure for me, as long as Mikey and I sat in the back seat all the way. My aunt Lillian had died and left a house in Tampa, which needed to be emptied out, cleaned, and prepared for sale. Since her sister, my dearest Gramma Rhoda, had been too old to handle these affairs, my mother stepped in, seeing it as an opportunity to give her children a wonderful trip she could otherwise not afford. My father encouraged us to go, although he could not join us. Having taught his son to drive a milk truck since Butch was fourteen years old, Dad had complete faith in the driving ability of his now twenty-two-year-old son and knew that he would happily relieve my mother any time she asked. We had two weeks to do it all, since my older brother had to return to college.

Planning the trip was exhilarating for me. Mom insisted that we see as many things and places as possible, both on the trip going south and back to our parochial city of Syracuse in Upstate New York. So we planned something for everybody: museums for Mom, petting zoos for Mikey, and amusement parks for all of us. Since there was no well-developed interstate system in 1962, much of our travel would take us through many rural Southern towns with two-lane roads. We had no idea at the time how foreign a world this would be for us "Yankees." "Thou preparest a table before me in the presence of mine enemies" (Psalm 23:5, KJV). This would be the first big trip of my life, although, I have to count the time two years before when I flew to Florida with my grandmother. She so desperately wanted to visit with her sister, yet she was terrified of flying. Her solution was to take me and her secret potion of Alka Seltzer with her. In those days Alka Seltzer came in cylinder-shaped glass bottles completely covered with the label. Now my grandmother was never ashamed to take a drink of "spirits" from time to time, but she had some rigid ideas about how a lady appears in public. Getting "snookered" on an airplane would not have fit in to those ideas.

Nevertheless, we were barely airborne before she asked the stewardess for some water for her Alka Seltzer, which the stewardess promptly delivered. My grandmother waited a short time and then surreptitiously poured a goodly amount of Windsor Canadian out of the Alka Seltzer bottle and into her tiny cup of water, all of this concealed by her large tapestry purse. This scene was repeated every fifteen minutes or so until the contents of the Alka Seltzer bottle disappeared. I was sure that the stewardess was thinking, "This woman's stomach is made of iron!" Fortunately, the potion had the expected effects, and my no longer nervous grandmother drifted off to sleep for the duration of the flight. As she slept and I grew accustomed to the rhythms of her "delicate," lady-like snoring, I wrote the first lines of my first poem, "Wonderland by Night." Although I was thrilled by my first flight, I didn't consider the trip much of an adventure, having spent all my time in the company of eighty-year-olds. This trip would be different.

I still recall the feeling of excitement as we piled our suitcases into the trunk of our old turquoise and white Buick Special with the three holes on the side. My dad had named her "Beauty," and my little brother often talked to her. Mikey and I loved the back seat because we got all the extra wind when the windows were down. Our first brief stop was in New York City, where I remember my mother whining about the traffic and trying to find a parking place. We had lunch at Mama Leone's, and I recall thinking how odd to place a statue of the Blessed Mother next to a half-naked Venus on the Half Shell. My mother said that's because Italian Americans are "eclectic," but I didn't know what that word meant yet. I *did* know that my neck was sore from looking up at all the skyscrapers. We went up on the top of the State Tower building, and Mikey kept chanting, "King Kong, King Kong, King Kong," until my mother threatened to slap him. Although we could not ascend the steps to the torch with our older brother, I recall standing in front of Our Lady Liberty and memorizing those wonderful words written by Emma Lazarus, "Give me your tired, your poor, your huddled masses yearning to breathe free / The wretched refuge of your teeming shore / Send these, the homeless, tempest tossed to me, I lift my lamp beside the Golden Door." Tears welled in my eyes as I thought about my other grandmother, who first saw that statue when she was just sixteen, like me, and I wondered if anyone had translated the words for her.

Butch insisted on crossing the Brooklyn Bridge because he had learned so much about it in his history class, so we too learned about how it was one of the oldest suspension bridges in the country, how its designer died of a tetanus infection, how many people died of something called "caisson disease" while building it, and how it was finally completed by a woman who carried a rooster across it on opening day. I liked the woman part, and Mikey liked the rooster part.

Mom wanted us to see Times Square and Central Park, which we did before crossing the Verrazano

Narrows Bridge heading south. Only two years later that bridge would have such special meaning for me.

Our next stop was Washington, D.C. In spite of Mikey's innumerable exclamations of, "Are we there yet?" I was absolutely awestruck, especially as my older brother explained and elaborated on the history and importance of each monument we visited. I especially enjoyed his story about why the goddess of justice was blindfolded. Mom kept teasing him about how his Catholic education had paid off, but I felt that my brother was expressing genuine pride and patriotism. I was sure that he would become a good lawyer.

We had so little time in the Smithsonian, which is where Mikey wanted to live for the rest of his life, but we did linger at the Lincoln Memorial, and I read the immortal words of the president's Gettysburg Address. This was almost a religious experience for me, standing in the shadow of so great, good, and brave a man, Abraham, who delivered our nation from the abomination of slavery. "He leadeth me in the paths of righteousness for His name's sake" (Psalm 23:2, KJV).

In spite of the oppressive heat, I could have stayed much longer in our nation's capitol, but time was pressing on us, and we had yet so far to go. I was struck by how much the terrain began to change once we left Virginia. There was no time this time to visit the great battlefields of the Civil War. Mikey and I feigned great interest as my brother shouted back to us about all the amazing things that happened here and there as we drove through.

I think we saw the first South of the Border sign when we entered North Carolina. This was how my mother dealt with Mikey's protests: "Read the mileage on the signs." He had no understanding of mileage, of course, but he did make a game out of counting the signs. Everyone knows that the South of the Border tourist attraction is what my Gramma Rhoda referred to as a "gip joint," yet something about it compels the traveler to stop and buy some "cheap junk." And so we did. Some lunch, some gas, a sticker for the car bumper, and some toys for Mikey took us about two hours. It took Mikey twenty minutes, back in the car, to break his toys.

My mother and brother congratulated each other on the good time they were making and decided we would stop for dinner at a Howard Johnson's and maybe even find a motel with a pool. This kept Mikey's mind occupied for a long time. We had made it almost all the way through South Carolina. I had just begun to mark the beautiful Spanish moss hanging from the trees, thinking how ethereal it looked (I knew that word from reading so much Poe). I also caught a few glimpses of the run down one-room shacks just off the highway. We had not yet seen any signs of segregation, or perhaps just didn't recognize them.

"He leadeth me beside the still waters" (Psalm 23:2, KJV). It was such a treat for the children of a milkman to stay in a motel with a pool. Butch relished in showing off his prowess at diving, and Mikey's refrains of, "Look at this, Mom," seemed never ending as he demonstrated his five-stroke technique. Never fond of swimming, I preferred to sit by the pool and watch rather than get my hair wet. We stayed poolside until Mikey looked like a prune and Butch had a nosebleed. Mom reminded us all that we had a long trip the next day through Georgia and that we would need to get up early.

Early was around eight in the morning, and we were starving. We stopped for gas at the nearest station, and that was really the first I saw of it. There were no black people around the station and none at the pumps, but there were two water fountains next to the one bathroom. The bathroom and one fountain had signs on them that read, "whites only," and they were both functional. The other fountain was filthy and did not work. I felt a certain, strange little tingling in my legs and decided not to get a drink here and to wait until I got to a restaurant to use the ladies' room. I said nothing to my mother.

We chose a roadside diner, which my mother judged to have real, home-cooked food. I was quite confused when the waitress asked me if I'd like my eggs "urp" and asked her to repeat what she had said.

"Urp. Ya'll know, sunny side urp."

I replied, "Scrambled, thank you." Mom said to be adventurous and try everything, so I took a shot at something called "grits," which reminded me of the time Butch stuffed wallpaper paste in my mouth. After this I vowed not to venture beyond Southern fried chicken. We saw no black people in this diner.

The daylong ride through Georgia was terribly hot and mostly uneventful, since we did not stop to see the roadside alligator farms. We did see lots and lots of Spanish moss hanging from the trees, many beautiful wildflowers growing along the road, signs to the peach groves, billboards advertising pecan pie at the next truck stop, and very many run-down shacks with beat-up old trucks parked next to them with the occasional black person sitting on the porch. Around noon, we had to stop in order to shut Mikey up and empty our bladders. Once again, Mom chose a diner and gas station, since that's about all there was, but this one had a few black people hanging around outside. I immediately asked for the bathrooms and was told they were around the back of the building. As a sixteen-year-old, northern girl who played basketball with black girlfriends, I was totally unprepared for what I saw. There were three doors: one marked ladies, one marked gentlemen, and one marked "niggers." I was standing there staring, almost able to visualize my friend Betty's beautiful black face when Butch came up behind me. He stared for a moment and then mumbled, "That ain't right, just ain't right. Man, I gotta take a leak," and went into the room marked "gentlemen." Like a zombie, I entered the room marked "ladies."

"What's wrong with you guys?" my mother asked over breakfast, since both my brother and I were very quiet. "You'll see when you go to the bathroom," was all we said. Later, when she got into the passenger side, indicating that it was my brother's turn to drive, she said, as if talking to herself more than to us, "I heard about this stuff. It's just so hard to believe until you actually see it."

She was soon interrupted by Mikey's inquiry, "Hey, Mom, what's a nigger?" We were all so grateful that he had waited until he got into the car to ask that question.

It had been a long, hot drive over the last four days, and we were anxious to get to the house in Tampa. I had remembered its lovely stucco, painted deep pink with a white awning over the front door, a couple of plastic flamingos on the lawn, and the intoxicating smell of the night blooming jasmine wafting from the backyard garden. I don't know what Mom and Butch were imagining, but none us expected what we saw.

It had been weeks since anyone cut the grass, so it was hard for us to even see the address on the house. "Wow! It's a jungle!" Mikey exclaimed. Butch found the stones that led to the front door and stomped the grass back to make a path for us. The moment Mom unlocked the door and started to open it, we all smelled the mildew within. A few huge beetles scurried away as we entered, and I shuddered, thinking, *This is where we sleep tonight?*

"Thy rod and thy staff, they comfort me" (Psalm 23:4, KJV). "Never mind, kids," my mother reassured us. "I've been a landlady and scrubwoman all my life. This doesn't scare me." Within hours, Butch was hacking and mowing the lawn, and Mom and I were wiping down the walls with bleach. We let Mikey open all the windows and rake up the grass clippings for Butch. We worked all day in the heat, except for the brief lunch break. Just as the cool of evening was coming on, we stepped out to admire Butch's handiwork. Mikey snuck up behind me and said, "Hey, sis, look what I found!" as he dropped a little green snake down the back of my blouse. Screaming as only a teenage girl can scream, I was jumping up and down hysterically, thinking it could be poisonous, but the snake slipped right through and slithered off almost invisibly into the freshly cut grass. Mikey was appropriately chastised and warned, which didn't dampen any of his ecstasy in watching my reaction.

When I was finally calmed down, we all went to the local grocery store and bought the fixings for a spaghetti supper, which was always our first choice when we were celebrating. It was also cheap. We happily cooked it on the nice clean stove, and that evening we drifted off into an exhausted sleep, carried away by the sweet fumes of night booming jasmine that crept into our open windows. "Thou anointed my head with oil; my cup runneth over" (Psalm 23:5, KJV).

It would be another two days until my mother was able to arrange things with my aunt Lillian's lawyer and secure a real estate agent. We continued working on the house to make it as attractive for sale as possible. This, of course, was incredibly boring for me, but almost unbearable for Mikey. Our only solace was my mother's promise that we would leave soon. She fired Mikey's imagination when she assured him that we were going on an adventure through the Everglades on an amazing flying boat, and that we would see alligators and huge spiders and snakes hanging out of trees. I wondered how she knew all this, since my mother had never traveled much, but she had read "every book in the branch library." She pacified me and my older brother with tales of the rich and famous we might see in Miami, but even more important, we would have a couple of days to just lie on the beach with fun and frolic in the ocean. "He restoreth my soul" (Psalm 23:3, KJV).

As children, our only affordable vacation was a few days in Atlantic City on the Jersey shore, if Gramma Rhoda came along. I used to be amazed at how Gramma pulled ten-dollar bills out of her bra, stockings, and sometimes even her girdle, but she had to go to the ladies room for that trick. She was the one who told me that every time I went on a date, I should have a ten-dollar bill stuffed in some secret, safe place, just in case. She never did say what the "just in case" was, but my girlfriends I and figured it out.

When the anxiously awaited moment finally came, my heart was filled with mixed emotions as we pulled away from the house, now beautifully cleaned, lovely and most presentable for the next lucky inhabitant. My aunt Lillian, like my Gramma Rhoda had always been a favorite of mine. They spoiled me, doted over me, warned me, and shared wondrous stories with me about their lives, their struggles as women in a world owned by men. They taught me all their passive-resistive techniques and all their dirty tricks. I loved their laughter and wisdom, and my poet's soul most adored their tragedies: poverty, hunger, stillbirth, divorce, and isolation. These women knew it all and triumphed over it. Most of all, they knew how to laugh, and they invited me to laugh with them. I remembered tying my aunt's long red and gray hair into braids while she told me those stories. She smelled of lavender. My grandmother smelled like roses, and my mother definitely smelled of lemon blossom. As anxious as I was for the next adventure, it was hard to let go of that house. I stared out the back window until we passed out of view, leaving the deep pink house with the night blooming jasmine forever.

The Everglades were everything my kid brother hoped they would be, and the stuffed alligator trophy my mother bought for him from the tourist gift shop sustained him all the way to Miami. The back seat of our Buick became the scene for endless swamp adventures filled with intrigue and impossible heroics, which inevitably ended in the destruction of the alligator. That poor alligator died so many times I felt relief for it when we arrived in Miami and I was able to make it go away somewhere in the motel. It was a modest place but only two blocks from the beach, and we were thrilled—two days, two wonderful days of lying on the beach and playing in the ocean. Oh, the taste of salt water! Oh, the thrill of casting the body into the tip of a wave and riding it home! Oh the deep, penetrating feel of the sun's rays on the skin, the vibrating heat emanating from the sand, and oh the sexy tan I would go home with to attract the imaginary seventeen-year-old lover! I had it all planned. "He maketh me to lie down in green pastures" (Psalm 23:2, KJV).

We packed our beach bags in anticipation of every possible outcome. My older brother seemed to disappear almost instantaneously, not to be found for hours. And so we passed the first twenty-four hours of fun-filled laughter, sun, and sand. None of us could have anticipated what was brewing for us only a hundred miles offshore.

At breakfast on the second day, my older brother busied himself with cheap imitations of Jewish accents, telling stupid jokes about "Mammie Bitch," which I gathered meant Miami Beach. Mikey was absorbed in nagging my mother to replace his stuffed alligator with a stuffed dolphin, and I was visualizing my sexy tan. My mother, ever the Taurus, was already thinking about the return trip home, which routes we could take, how much time we could squeeze out, how much money was left.

Who can describe the mix of enjoyment and melancholy one experiences on the last day or last hour of any special moment or occasion in time? There's a certain desperation to hurry up and enjoy, absorb every last bit, every second, until it's hardly pleasurable anymore. And when the agony and the ecstasy are over, one admittedly feels relief. We had all read the signs saying, "Swim at your own risk," but because there were lifeguards on duty, we abandoned ourselves to the reverie of the moment, each to his own.

Butch was the first to "hit the water" that day. Mom was busy with a magazine, and I settled into a schedule of fifteen minutes on each side in an attempt to get a nice, even tan. Boy! I was going to look good in September. Maybe some boy would even notice me.

None of us would remember, or maybe never even bothered to ask how it was that Mikey got hold of a surfboard that day, but he did. And there he was suddenly having the time of his young life. There's no way he could have understood how important it was for a young "stud" like his older brother to have a surfboard to impress the girls. Mom and I watched, fully in maternal gear, from the shore. Butch's radar somehow zeroed in on the kid's surfboard. There was a brief and hopeless struggle; Butch emerged with the surfboard and took off for parts unknown; Mikey was left in the salty distance.

Life presents us with so many questions that we struggle to understand long after events have transpired. My mother was an excellent swimmer. Why she sent me out to bring Mikey back, neither of us would ever understand. To me, it was very understandable that I was angry as a bag of hornets. I was only halfway through my tanning timetable, but I was also a dutiful and respectful young woman in spite of the fact that, in my young mind, my mother was an idiot. So, in my anger, I did what I was taught not to do in my YWCA swimming classes. I swam out to sea. Besides, from the shore, I could see that Mikey was only waist deep in water. I wanted to hurry and get back, even if I had to drag him, being the unreasonable nine-year-old that he was.

I remember how strange it was, the ease with which I reached him. It was a long distance out to him, and I would have thought it would take me longer to get to him than it did. Nevertheless, as a weak swimmer who had to keep her head above water, I was pretty tired by the time I reached him and ever so happy to lower my feet and touch the sand. The water was about to my hips and Mikey's shoulders. He did not, of course, want to get out of the water. I figured I could cajole him by promising to teach him how to body surf. I showed him how to put his arms out in front of him and instructed him to jump just in front of the next wave. "I'll be right behind you," I assured him.

What happened next has always been a real blur in my mind, and yet, at the same time the most crystalline, clairvoyant, and intensely truthful experience of my entire life, either before or after. Perhaps the wave was a little bigger than I had anticipated; surely the current was, and I should have known we were standing on a sandbar. I know for sure that I was clinically conscious through much of this—the rest is inexplicable.

The wave nearly knocked us senseless, and when both our heads bopped up to the surface, I realized that Mikey had been pulled quite far away from me and that the current was working against us. I could not get to him. All I could think to do was scream, "Swim, Mikey! For God sake's, honey, swim! Swim with all your might! Try to get to the shore!" Then, I started to scream for help, my arms flailing wildly, trying to keep my head above water. I vaguely remember hearing my mother's terrified screams and pleas as she ran into the water. "Help, oh God, somebody please help me," were the last words I heard her say. Some enormous power surged up in me. I felt like an electrical charge was racing through my veins. I felt suddenly huge, powerful, invincible! I saw a young couple on a surfboard racing toward me. I pushed them away, screaming, "Get my little brother! He can't swim! I'll be all right." I watched as they scrambled across the waves, so much water splashing that I could barely see them lift Mikey onto their board. It was then that I knew I was not all right. Alone and drifting further out to sea, I strained for the last of my strength, and another wave struck me. "Yea, though I walk through the Valley of the Shadow of Death, I will fear no evil, for thou art with me" (Psalm 23:4, KJV).

It was green, deeply, intensely, vibrating, pulsating, endless shades of green; green on every side, all around and within, all shades emanating simultaneously. I understood then that I was not "seeing" green, but that I was "being" green. I was in the green, a part of it, contained and sustained in it. I felt myself shedding that last bit of energy like "taking off" my body, dropping it, and letting it drift with the current. Oh, the relief! I became aware of a strange sense of looking down, and there I saw my body, limp and curled over, almost in a fetal position, floating calmly in the water. I understood that I was no longer in it, but rather than being shocked, frightened, or confused, I remember thinking, "Oh, I'm dying…and it's not what I thought. It's not the way they taught me."

In the same way that the green approached me, there was music, but not like anything on earth. Tradition would call it the voices of the angels, but that's too simple. Yes, I could tell they were voices, and yes, I could tell they were not human. The tone, the range, the dimension, the music added up to an overwhelming, penetrating, permeating sense of peace. I not so much heard but rather "felt" the music, and once again, I heard my own thoughts. *I am going home. I am going home,* and it felt *so good.* With that thought, I was pulled in a direction, toward a great softly glowing light, which seemed, proverbially, at the end of a long tunnel. I no longer felt alone but was keenly aware of a "presence" that was guiding me through this tunnel which was very dark, cold, and scary along its perimeters. If I had to describe this presence, I could only say, "Love."

"Love" stayed with me, and we seemed to float until I encountered a kind of barrier, a "wall" perhaps over which I could "peek" inside. Oh, the shimmering beauty, the peace, the joy! I had forgotten Mikey, Butch, and even Mom. I cared not about the imaginary seventeen-year-old lover, or the golden tan, or anything on earth. I wanted only one thing, and that was to go inside that place. I wanted to go home. Clearly, I didn't get there. I remember ever so gently being shown something, and then I knew I had a choice that I had to make.

That's the part that's hard to explain to people, the so-called "unconscious" part. As soon as I knew I could make a choice, I was consciously aware of a very fat man in a red polka-dot bathing suit dragging me through the surf, to the shore, struggling to avoid my swinging arms and ignoring my screams of, "Let me go!" He must have thought my brain was water logged when I kept hollering, "No, no, I want to go back!" I was barely on my feet when Mikey came running at me in tears. "Magee, oh Magee, it's Mom. Is she gonna die?" Two lifeguards knelt over my mother's listless body, one pumping, and one breathing. I recognized what they were doing from my YWCA training. Now, I was fully conscious of the fact that I was back in the world, perhaps without a mother. I know it's a cliché, but it did seem like an eternity until she coughed up a mouthful of salt water and mumbled, "Mikey, my Mikey." It was the first time in my life that I was to know the hell of feeling helpless. It was just about this time that Butch showed up, still carrying the surfboard and wondering what was going on. The fat man in the red polka-dot suit disappeared. I thought I was supposed to thank him, but he was nowhere to be found.

I honestly don't remember much of the return trip home. I don't think we stopped many places, all of us so absorbed in our thoughts, being so anxious to get back home to Dad, to the family, to a normal life. But my mother and I would never be "normal" again. Her trip into the green was a little different than mine yet essentially the same. We talked about it together a lot, but not with strangers. Although we were thrilled to be alive and vowed to live our lives more fully, we were never again afraid of death. Many wonderfully lived years later, as I stood beside her bed and held her hand, her last words to me were, "Don't cry, honey. I'm going home."

I now believe that what I saw at the wall was all the unfinished work that lay ahead of me for the next sixty or so earth years. I looked at the face of death several times since that watery awakening and ended up making the same choice. "Surely goodness and mercy shall follow me all the days of my life" (Psalm 23:6, KJV). Indeed, it's been a wonderful life full of goodness and mercy, love, work, challenges, awards, triumphs, tests, victories, and faith. Yet I've been waiting since I was sixteen to "dwell in the house of the Lord forever" (Psalm 23:6, KJV). I too want to go home.

JOSHUA, "GIFT OF GOD"

His name was Charlie, and he carried his whole world in his arms. By the end of the day, my husband and I would forever refer to him as Atlas, because he carried the weight of the world upon his shoulders. He was only nineteen years old.

It was early summer, Memorial weekend as I recall. We had gotten up at an ungodly hour for a Saturday morning— six o'clock—but we were very excited about going sailing for the weekend. My brother had just taken delivery on a thirty-two-foot catch-rigged beauty named *Satisfaction*. She was red, white, and blue with a glorious spinnaker that ballooned like a parachute. We had such visions of wind-worshiping ecstasy. I even bought special sailing clothes and shoes for the weekend. I thought it was important to have the right things to wear. We were ready!

The weather was beautiful—eighty degrees, clear skies, winds around ten to fifteen knots, an absolute sailor's delight! "Sail away, sail away," we kept singing that morning as we threw our things into our newly purchased waterproof duffel bags, gobbled a quick breakfast of bagels and cream cheese, and gulped down lots of black coffee.

We were married less than a year, and our only child was our darling, drooling, one hundred and eighty-nine pound, bouncing baby boy. It wasn't easy waking Goliath. Saint Bernards are known to be good sleepers. They sleep almost as much as they drool, but this dog took the world prize for sleeping. We should have named him Somnolus, the Greek god of sleep.

To me, he was absolutely beautiful! I bought him as a pup, in my desperate days of female single life and when my maternal clock was ticking. I had to have something to cuddle, care for, nurture, and pamper. My arms were empty. And for all the blessings in my life, I was still left feeling somehow yearning.

Goliath helped me deal with that profoundly empty feeling. I trained him from peeing on papers to winning blue-ribbon prizes for "Best in Show." Goliath was my companion, my friend, my confidant, and the only faithful man I had known until I met my husband. Needless to say, certain arrangements had to be made to accommodate my child, things like a bare-based van to drive him around in, which also served well for hauling cargo. It was a white and olive Chevy box with wheels, and it served its function very well.

By seven forty-five in the morning, we had all our gear, clothes, food, and Saint Bernard safely assembled in the "Slobberwagon," our name for Goliath's van. I have spent most of my life complaining about having to get up early, yet I treasure the exquisite sense of morning, the slightly sticky feel of morning air, which smells of more ozone than any other time of day. Breathing in the morning air is like drinking orange juice. It somehow kicks the body machine into motion, suddenly awakening cells and stretching limbs, and the life force unfolds as a flower meeting the sun. It's especially delicious on a morning when you voluntarily get up early. Likewise, morning colors are softly vivid, delightfully pastel pinks, blues, and peaches, locked in the mist of first light—eye candy that sticks to the brain.

Goliath settled on the bench seat behind our two-bucket seats and immediately went to sleep. We were only three blocks from home when we could hear the steady rhythm of his jowls as they rose and fell with his sleepy breathing. The tired little town whose best claim to fame was the Women's Suffrage Convention in 1848 was just beginning to rise. Two, maybe three, people were walking along Main Street. The gas station on Routes 5 and 20, two of America's most scenic highways, was gearing up for the day's business.

We stopped to fill up the tank, selected a few snacks such as Tasty Cakes, peanuts, and Goliath's favorite—cheese twists—and headed for Syracuse, where we could pick up Route 81 North and head for Sackett's Harbor on Lake Ontario. We were anticipating a glorious sail, crossing to Kingston, Ontario, in Canada.

The half hour or so to reach Route 81 was uneventful as the dog slept in the back, and Jack and I were still too tired to talk much. We didn't really notice the dingy slums of the south side of Syracuse as we passed through, so changed now from the blue-collar neighborhood in which I had grown up. We were not cognizant of the great white dome of the Syracuse University Athletic Program, and took the sprawling Upstate Medical Center for granted.

There is a complex network of highway where routes 81, 481, 90, and 690 come together near the medical center. It reminds me of the complex knots I tried to learn when I was a Girl Scout. We had just cleared our way through it to reach 81 North when, out of the corner of my half-open right eye, I noticed a junky old car broken down on the right shoulder, its hood standing up at attention, waving for help, steam slipping out as an afterthought.

We were traveling at fifty-five, maybe sixty miles per hour when we passed. The man and child on the side of the road were a momentary illusion. We were probably a quarter mile past them when in my still sleepy stupor I said, "Jack, I think that man on the side of the road was holding a baby." He said nothing in response but immediately slowed down and pulled to a stop on the shoulder of the road. It's a precarious exercise to back up a quarter mile on the shoulder of a major American highway. Just trying to keep on a straight path takes two people—a driver and a navigator.

Charlie was quick to notice that we had stopped for him and came running toward us as quickly as he could, given the bundle in his arms. We stopped moving when he neared us, oblivious to the now-zooming traffic headed north on 81. Goliath lifted his head ever so slightly, mildly aware of some obligation to do something.

"Thank you, thank you," he repeated as we met. "I'm Charlie Wright, and this is my son, Josh. It means 'gift of God' in Hebrew. Thank you so much for stopping for us. Thank you. Thank you."

In less than sixty seconds, we learned that the old car had blown a piston, that Josh had had a chemo therapy treatment for his leukemia, and that he was headed home to Pulaski to his seventeen-year-old wife and his family, who anxiously waited for them. I knew Pulaski, its beautiful salmon stream, its inlets leading to the great Ontario, its terrible winters, its simple people, its poverty, the one restaurant in town that served deep-fried mushrooms, as if they knew I was coming.

My mother spent her summers in Pulaski with her father, an eccentric part-time inventor and part-time ne'er-do-well. My mama knew every inch of the Salmon River, and when we kids were little, she often rented a rowboat, took us out, and told us wonderful stories of her adventures as she tried to escape her stepmother. She had a falling out with her father sometime after she married my dad, and they never spoke, nor met again until Grandpa's death just two years before my marriage. Yet Mama always let, indeed encouraged, me to go visit Gramps when I was staying with my cousins. My uncle always remained close to his dad and frequently took some of his eight kids, with me in tow, to visit the strange old inventor who loved to tinker on his beautiful Chris Craft boats but never took them out of the river. He couldn't swim, and he feared the water.

My grandfather was an amazing man, a brilliant inventor, creating one of the first rotary engines and one of the first air compressors. Sometimes he would apply for a patent, sometimes he wouldn't. Mama said he was much too scarred by the Great Depression and feared success, but he did know how to live with hardship.

My uncle was like that too. He made good money as a tool and dye maker, but he kept his family always on the edge of poverty. As I grew older and realized how much more material wealth I had than my cousins, I often wondered why. I loved to visit my cousins, and I adored my uncle. He seemed to know everything; he told us children wonderful stories, and he was fun to be with, but we had to sleep together in one bed, and we had to eat the food that the farmers at farmers' market sold at discount, just before packing up. My cousins always ate hamburger meat, never steak. My cousins didn't visit my house so much. They were afraid of Uncle Johnny when he got drunk. Despite all this, both families found ways to bridge our differences. When I was with my uncle, I learned things my father never had time to teach me, and when my cousins were with us, they went to restaurants and other places their father would never take them. It seemed to mean so much to them that they would even make a game of hiding in the closet with me when my father was on a rage, until he went to bed. Both of our families went camping together in the summer. I look back and wonder, *How?*

"We're headed that way," we told Charlie, and it wouldn't be any trouble at all to take a little detour off to old exit 35. Then he could get the baby home to its mama and come back with some friends to tow the car. He seemed amazed that we would do this for him.

"It's the way I was raised," I said.

"But I didn't think city folk were like that, "he said. That's when I told him I knew Pulaski.

He was a little apprehensive when we opened the side panel doors and he saw the great dog. "Man's best friend," my husband said and directed the big dog to his blanket in the back of the van. It was all the same to Goliath—another place to sleep.

I stood watching, studying, as Charlie ever so gingerly climbed onto the bench seat, balancing the delicate little bundle in his arms. I climbed in after and helped him buckle in as my husband secured the doors and walked to the driver's seat. The baby was awake, though very quiet, and I caught a glimpse of his pasty, gray complexion, so unnatural looking for an infant. His little face was thin and drawn, his corn silk brown hair scattered in little patches on his head. His sparkling eyes were the only light in his little face. He seemed to me like one of those Keene paintings of the sad children with the huge, cat-like eyes. His father held a bottle to his mouth, which Josh held between his lips but did not suck. He never made a sound the whole trip.

The hour's drive to the Pulaski exit seemed to go by quickly as Charlie and I exchanged stories of childhood memories in that dingy little town with its glorious river. His father knew my grandfather, and he knew my mother's half brother—now the sheriff of the river. We talked about how good the pike taste fresh out of the water and just how best to cook them, and how the town explodes and comes alive when the salmon run starts, and how the fishermen come from all over the world. We talked of family campouts at Selkirk State Park and getting drunk on Saturday nights at Rainbow Shores, and just how good it was to be with friends and sing along with the jukebox. He understood when I told him about that incredible, indescribable feeling of standing on the rocky shore, looking across all that watery space, especially at night with a full moon, and imagining that there was some Canadian person standing on the other side imagining too.

After forty miles, we were like family. Farms around Pulaski are generally very flat, wide-open spaces that invite the winter winds to rip, tear, and howl like a band of banshees. The dirt road leading up to Charlie's house was a typical, nondescript farm road, a decent stretch off the main. The first glimpse of the homestead told that these were very poor people. There was a rusty old tractor, whose paint was chipped and faded, parked next to the barn. Both barn and house needed many repairs. The roofs were pocked with makeshift, temporary patches. The wooden planks of the house were brittle and worn gray with weathering, so dry they seemed to be gasping for drink.

The morning's laundry was hung on a line tied across two scraggly, stubborn trees in the front yard. Sheets and trousers moved sluggishly in the morning's breeze, keeping themselves busy while waiting, the way a worried friend paces the room, taps the fingers, cracks the knuckles. An outhouse and a well pump stood silently between the house and barn.

Out of the mouth of this gloomy cavern, through a squeaky screen door, burst forth one of the most beautiful young women, still a girl actually, that I had ever seen outside of *Seventeen Magazine*. Her hair was silky, shoulder length, straight, and honey blonde. It bounced left and right as she ran to accept her child. It seemed as if she flew off the two or three steps of the decrepit porch. Charlie, momentarily unconscious of our presence, delicately transferred the infant, who seemed to flow into his mother's arms. Her welkin eyes turned liquid, a few tears of relief dripped down an ivory cheek punctuated here and there with pale tan freckles. She kissed the child gently on the brow and turned to enter the house as if she had seen no one but her baby.

She had been followed out of the house by two women and a man, clearly in their forties, maybe fifties, two young women who looked very much like their sister, two tall, awkward young men, and a medium-sized dog of some vaguely beagle origin. It was a gentle beast with floppy ears and soft brown eyes that lent to its pathetic expression. I started for a moment, thinking of Goliath in the van, but he was never a fighter. Besides, he was still asleep.

We never did see young Mary Anne again, but Charlie quickly introduced us to his mother, father, aunt June, brothers, Johnny and Paul, sisters-in-law, Betsy and Jeannie, and dog, "Honker." He explained our presence in endlessly grateful terms, and we were led, somewhat reluctantly, into their humble home. It was clean in the kitchen, and something wonderful was cooking on the stove, something wafting of chicken and corn. They offered us chairs at the kitchen table while the rest of the family stood along the kitchen walls. All six chairs were different designs; I chose a Victorian design, and Jack chose a Windsor. Mrs. Wright invited us to stay for lunch, but we assured her that we had obligations.

"Surely we can offer you something for your kindness!" Mr. Wright exclaimed.

"Well, maybe some water for our dog," my husband suggested.

"Great!" the man replied and left the kitchen just as Aunt June pulled the cornbread out of the oven. It was buttered and placed in front of us, still steaming, before we could protest. It was as good a slice of cornbread as I had ever tasted, especially when washed down with cold, creamy, whole milk.

By the time we had finished, and the brothers and sisters briefly chatted with us about Syracuse, Pulaski, and Sackett's Harbor, Mr. Wright returned to the kitchen bearing two plastic gallon jugs, one in each hand, and a large, bulky, brown grocery bag tucked under his armpit.

"Best water in the county," he boasted. "No chemicals, no impurities. It comes from real deep. That's why it's cold. Thought your little fella might enjoy these too," he explained as he handed Jack the bag full of medium-sized dog biscuits. Mr. Wright had not seen Goliath. I suppose he thought this bag full a generous supply. I thought of poor Honker going without for a week while Goliath made a mere snack out of the whole bag full.

Charlie and his brothers were discussing plans on how to retrieve the old car as we prepared to say our good-byes. Everyone but Mary Anne and Josh accompanied us back to the van amid copious sayings of, "God bless you," "have a safe trip," and "thank you again." By this time, Goliath was sitting up on the bench seat and curiously surveying the environs. I noticed the sinking expression on Mr. Wright's face as he saw "the little fella."

Impulsively, Charlie threw his arms around me and held me very tightly for what seemed a long time. Then, he grabbed my husband's right hand, which almost instantaneously evolved into a manly bear hug. "You're good people," he said, clearly fighting a sob.

Once back in the van, we silently, mechanically arranged the water gallons, tucked the biscuits safely out of Goliath's reach, buckled up, and slowly pulled out of the drive, dragging our hearts behind us in the dust.

It took us about forty minutes more to find the slip at Sackett's Harbor, where floated the *Satisfaction*, awaiting our glamorous arrival. We said nothing to each other on the trip from the Wright farm to our destination, save words of direction on how to get there and initial unloading and embarking procedures. It was all business now; we seemed to have misplaced our anticipation, and I felt very uncomfortable in my designer sailing outfit. We longed for a noisy arrival.

With brief apologies for our two-hour delay, we quickly boarded our vessel, carefully guiding Goliath up the gangplank. I secured his life jacket and tethered him to a cleat on the deck of the bow. With the gentle breeze blowing through his long, black-white-tan hair, he seemed quite awake now and ready for the adventure. I gave him a handful of Mr. Wright's biscuits to keep him busy while I helped to lift the sails and make ready for the crossing to Kingston.

I have always particularly enjoyed the raising of the sails. My brother, ever the anal pragmatist, and the frightened sailor, would ease his way out of harbor under gentle motor far beyond what reason would demand. But he was a lawyer, and I always understood the need for the lawyer's analytical skills. I, on the other hand, was the stupid, daring free spirit. I loved and respected my brother, but I wanted—I lusted—

for the wind! When the rags went up and filled with wind, I felt my spirit move. My soul told me in that instant that I could do anything, be anything, go anywhere! I looked at the great dog, his jowls flapping with the wind, and we were one soul bound together on a great ride through space and time. The dog and I read the wind, rode the wind, and breathed the wind.

It was easing into afternoon. We knew that with the promising good wind we could make it to the Kingston Harbor around sunset or shortly thereafter. Nothing else mattered now, not my brother's practice, not my students, my husband's sales, not even a poor family in Pulaski.

What mattered was the trim on the sails, just the right angle to catch the wind, the feel of the wind in the hair and across the skin, the splash of water across the bow, the creak of the halyards, the sun in the sky, the blessed people on board, the food we packed, the dear, willing dog, and the anticipation of a good meal and a fine wine at the Holiday Inn, once everything was tied down and secured.

One of the greatest lessons of life is that nothing goes according to plan. It was a fine sail, full of pleasure and opportunity for thought, but a sailor learns early that nature rules. She was kind to us on this trip, but her time schedule was a little different than ours. At the onset of sunset, when the sky was ablaze in red, orange, and gold, we were three-fourths of the way to our destination. We gathered in the pit, that is, where the captain steered the wheel, and made our plans for a nighttime "landing." We were well versed in this, and everyone was confident in what to do. Even Goliath seemed to know his role. We would be coming in under lights and motor, sails down and packed away. All we had to do then was to enjoy the interim.

The interim was everything. Having packed the sails, kissed the husband sharing the steering with his brother-in-law, secured the galley, and double-checked with everyone on board that they had their life jackets either on or close by, I took up my position on the bow next to my dear, hairy friend. Goliath and I, at least for the time being, owned the bow of our ship. My beautiful one-hundred-and-eighty-nine pound baby boy was sitting on his hinds, head held high, slobber frothing in the wind.

By now it was well into the sunset. Sunsets, for those who pay attention, are always miracles taken for granted. A young soldier once told me in a poem that sunsets are lessons, opportunities. They are the reflections of all the world's longing, aspirations, hopes, sorrows, and prayers, all painted on the sky. Sailors love sunsets, but I wonder how many read them that way.

Goliath and I sat in the bow, me with my arms wrapped about him, wind in our hair, as the great burning, crimson disk slipped slowly but steadily beneath the horizon. Things faded from brilliant to soft and misty, from light to dark, from clear to obscure.

It was as the last sliver of light slipped beneath the waves that we approached the safety and comfort of Kingston Harbor. In another moment or two, I'd have to leave the dog and grab the lines to secure the *Satisfaction* for the night. Ever so slowly, as one bends on knee to pray, my Goliath lowered his great body and laid his head down upon his front paws. He let out a plaintiff whine such as I had never before heard from him. I lay down, my face next to his, put my arms around his haunches, and let my tears roll onto his jowls. Caught in this final moment between last light and darkness, the dog and I both knew that in that moment, the soul of little Joshua Wright had returned to God.

BABA

This woman lived to make pierogi! "Yeet, yeet. You don yeet, you don lub it me!" she always said as she passed out the deep bowls of potatoes, sauerkraut, and prunes, wrapped in boiled dough and drowned in sautéed onions, swimming in butter and garlic, with just a touch of the occasional parsley. Oh God, the aroma! I can still smell it. It permeated the whole house, and it remains forever one of my most treasured childhood impressions.

Julie Patela was sixteen years old when her uncle returned from the United States of America in 1906 to a small Ukrainian village at the foot of the Ural Mountains. His mission was to bring his last remaining young relative to the New World, the Land of Opportunity.

Julia grew up on a sliver of farmland that stretched in a narrow strip up to the timberline. It defined her world as a destitute, hopeless place of subjugation. She went barefoot among the animals and the fields in the summer and wrapped hides and rags around her feet and legs, bound with strips of hide, to stay warm in winter. Shoes did not exist. Work was all she knew. Her shelter was a long hall of clay and stone, which included the family living quarters and the "barn" for the animals. For heat and cooling, the roof was covered with the rich, black soil that defined the "bread basket" of Eastern Europe. The oven, a clay mound that was the center point of her childhood home, often served as her bed, because the clay retained the heat. This was a favored spot for the children to cuddle together at night in the terrible winter. When fuel was scarce, or had completely run out, the family bedded down with the animals for warmth. "Da straw, it eez goot and varm," she said.

My baba (grandmother) told me it was difficult to travel from her village because no one had any shoes, wagons were few and far between and necessary for farm work, and also, peasants were fair game for the "fancy people" (aristocrats). Peasants who dared the roads were often intentionally run over, run down, killed, or injured for sport.

When I was old enough to perceive the prejudices of people around me, I became aware of what I thought was a remarkable aspect of my grandmother. She loved Jews! I mean, this woman would go to war to defend Jews. This was inconsistent with my other impressions of her. It would take years to understand this, but it had to do with reading. Julia, who became quite proficient in English as well as her native language, never learned to read or write. She understood this to be a great deprivation that had befallen her. "Ven I vas da little girl," she said, "dey came vid der books, and dey read to us, dos vonderful stories." She was speaking, as I later learned, of traveling bands of Jews who, like the gypsies, made their way from village to village, earning what they could. These Jews opened a door of wonder, imagination, and belief in possibility for my grandmother that she clung to until her dying day.

Steel plants were opening in the great cities of America. Miners were also needed, along with servants for the *noveau riche*. There seemed no end to opportunity in the New World and no hope in the Old. All one had to do was find out how to pay for passage. Julia's brothers and uncles had preceded her; a couple of brothers had found work in factories, and one aunt as a house servant in the great American Midwestern city of Chicago. Families worked together to save money and bring more family to this new world. Julia was among the last, perhaps because she was so young, but probably more importantly, she was her mother's last child. Mother Patela was never going to leave the Old World. She was old, and she was sick, very sick.

As a child, I was often frightened, alienated from my baba, because she seemed so "hard" to me. She was intimidating, aloof, perhaps even cold. She scared me. When I looked at her face sometimes, I thought she looked more like a man than a woman, so hard were her features. Her large, robust body was all strapped up in corsets, and her shortly cropped hair was wrapped in very tightly permed, little, white ringlets close to her scalp. I thought she thundered as she stomped around in her EnaJettic shoes, her stockings rolled down to the knee and held with garters. Once, when she was pounding the dough to make our coveted pierogies, for which my childhood stomach leaped in anticipation, I noticed her hands flying through the flour.

They were really strong, not delicate like my English grandmother's milky white hands with perfectly shaped nails all painted in red. Baba's hands were what my father called "the work horse hands." Indeed, her hands looked like my father's, thick, calloused, a little gnarled, and almost the same size.

As an adult, in one incredibly enlightened moment when my brothers and I interviewed and taped her as she served us endless bowls of pierogie drenched in sour cream, she grabbed me by the guts and tore me back into her time. She was just ninety-two and still recovering after her second brain surgery. We feared that we would lose our heritage if we didn't somehow record her life. She was generous enough to agree, in the name of love for her grandchildren, if only we would eat the pierogie she made for us.

"I vas so scared," she started. Who knows how long it was later when she had us all in tears, my usually ravenous brothers unable to swallow their pierogie. In her simple crude and direct English, she took us back to that awful day in her little village as her uncle waited beside the hand-drawn cart, with her very first pair of shoes strewn over his shoulders while she said her final farewell to her dying mother. They both knew they would never meet again. At sixteen, illiterate and heart-broken yet filled with adventure and anticipation, my grandmother knew she was burning every bridge behind her. There was only one direction to go, and that was forward to the West, to follow the sun.

I watched intently, the hard-scarred face of that old woman I had known all my life. The surface of her countenance reminded me of beautifully leather-bound collections of the world's great literary master-pieces. I was not prepared for the overwhelming rush of emotion that came in that moment of her remembrance, or "rembrance" she would say, never having mastered certain inflections of her new language. To this day, and as long as I live, I will wonder how the human spirit prevails. I am haunted by the apparition of a mother saying good-bye forever to a treasured child, sending her off to the absolute unknown. I am tortured by the fear of an adolescent child torn from all the security she has ever known, tossed into the absolute unknown. I shall never forget, as long as I live, the slowly trickling tears sliding down the wrinkled furrows of my grandmother's aged face, giving this to us, her dear prodigy, at immeasurable cost, the pain as fresh as it was seventy-six years prior.

Julia left her country with her uncle, wearing her first pair of shoes, tagging behind a hand-drawn cart all the way across Eastern Europe to a port in Italy. There they were able to sell the cart, add that money to their reserves, and book passage on a freighter bound for New York City, their ultimate goal being to meet up with relatives in Chicago. There, Julia could begin a new life of boundless opportunity.

"Plan all you vant," she said, "nuting ever goes da vay you tink it vill." The crossing was relatively uneventful, sticking close to her uncle. "I vas like da crazy glue to Vanya. He coun't even piss vitout me!" She giggled in "rembrance." In 1902, she could not speak a word of English. After they got through customs and boarded the trains heading north and then west, Uncle Vanya thought best to pin a note on Julia's jacket just in case they got separated. It was crude English, but it did contain a name and address.

It was to be a brief stop in Syracuse, just long enough to discharge and embark passengers and cargo. Uncle Vanya was fast asleep, exhausted from his journey. She didn't want to disturb him, and having used the ladies' rooms in the terminals at least three times already, Julia was sure she could find her way. At ninety-two she reminded those of us who had just become parents that all sixteen-year-olds believe that they can do more than they think they can. Having raised seven children of her own, and helping with grandchildren, we conceded that she knew what she was talking about.

The train was already about twenty miles out of the terminal when she returned to the track. The reality of it hit her in an instant. "I vas, how you say crazy voman, screaming, screaming for my uncle and my mama."

My baba was always a very religious person who taught all of us to believe and accept God's will. "He knows vat He eez doing, vhen you don't." When we asked, stupidly, why God lets people suffer, she would always answer with her Slavic stoicism, "Eez goot to suffer!" She meant, of course, that experience builds character, and faith in God will get you through anything.

Now it so happened that there was a relatively large Ukrainian community in Syracuse at the time. A porter, who came from a village not far from my grandmother's, approached her and spoke reassuringly in her native language. "It will be all right. I will help you," he told her in those heavy, slurring sounds that were always so mystifying to me, like magical incantations. He took her to his home, where she helped him care for his ailing wife while he attempted to find her relatives in Chicago. At the turn of the century, and with limited resources, these things took time. "Perhaps a month or two," he told her.

We have never been too certain how willing this man was to let his new, free house servant go, but no matter. Julia had found a church to attend where everyone spoke her language, barring a few strange accents. It was late summer now, and Saint John the Baptist's Holy Ukrainian Orthodox Church was having its annual picnic. "It vas God's plan, and oh it vas vonderful, I rember!"

Michael Lischak had just turned nineteen that summer. He was not so tall, but tall enough, handsome with that special, chiseled face that Slavic peoples have. He had a shock of thick, black, wavy hair and sparkling eyes that reflected great intelligence and ambition. He couldn't take those eyes off young Julia. When the polka band started, he extended his hand to her, the largest hand she had ever seen. She took it and danced with him for almost fifty years. They had nine children, seven of whom survived. "Gigi" (grandfather) always had several enterprises going at once, but when he won a small farm in Lafayette in a card game, he became a successful farmer and even ran a small dairy, teaching his oldest surviving son, my father, everything he knew.

The twenties and the thirties on the farm were not easy; money was hard to come by, but Prohibition offered an opportunity for an enterprising farmer whose young son loved to drive real fast. They never did get caught, and Grandpa was able to increase the size of the herd substantially. Unfortunately, Gigi took to drinking the product, very heavy drinking, which led to bouts of beatings. The younger children hid in the fields, and my baba took rat poison. She was a long time in the hospital while my father and mother cared for the younger children. When she came home, the beatings stopped, but not the drinking. Grandpa spent a lot of time in the barn with his two great draft horses, his beloved Mike and Pete.

The war came and took every man but my father off the farm. By now, my dad had a small milk delivery route and a son of his own. He found it very hard to help Grandpa. "But God eez goot, and I prayed and prayed He bring me back my boys." They all came back, my uncles: John, Walter, Macky, Alphonse, Joe, and "Billy," my baba's baby. They were changed, my mother said, different, distant, but I never noticed that when we gathered through the years to celebrate and eat tons of Baba's pierogies. They all seemed fine to me, except they drank a lot; all but Walter, who was a Jehovah's Witness, and young Billy, who was the first to go to college.

The family, including my baba, often spoke of Michael with mixed feelings. My second brother was named for him. I never knew my "grandpa with the big hands." My mother loved him dearly. I think my father never forgave himself for not stopping to check on his dad as he left the farm that evening. Dad looked down the road and saw Gigi leaning against the barn, his wagon and horses standing by. "I thought he was pissing is all," my father said through the years.

They found him late that night, lying in the fields. He had been drinking, fell off the wagon, and poor Pete could not help but step on Gigi's chest. Such a strong man, my grandfather took a week to die. Baba sold the farm and took a job as a cleaning woman in a local bank, where she worked until she was almost eighty. She lived with her various daughters, switching from time to time, but no matter where she lived, it was always at Baba's house that we gathered for Christmas and Easter to eat pierogies. I loved those gatherings with all my aunts and uncles and most especially my cousins! I miss them terribly, and thank God, and my baba, that I ever had them.

Yes, she was a hard woman; she had to be. I am haunted by a vision I once had of her. She was staying over at our house the night before she was to take me on a novena to a shrine in Canada. I was about fifteen at the time. She had laid down "for von moment" beside my sleeping father and slipped into sleep herself. When I went to wake her, their faces lay side by side on the big bed, and in the subdued light, I thought I was seeing double. What I saw was a mother and child, and I think it was then that I began to see the softer side of my grandmother, that I began to understand her great capacity for love.

Although Baba was always at the center of our lives, cooking and serving and shouting, "Yeet, yeet, you don yeet, you don lub it me," I never really knew her until my brothers and I made the tape recording. I guess I took for granted that she would always be there, cooking for us, giving the little surprise gifts to us and the grandchildren, taking pictures with the family for "rembrance." It was less than a year after that special Sunday afternoon in my aunt Mary's dining room, Baba stuffing pierogies into my brothers while I kept changing tapes, that she decided it was time. She returned to God, a servant whose work was well done, at the age of ninety-two. My father followed her only two years later.

DELIVERING SANTA CLAUS

Everybody loved him! What's not to love? It wasn't until he died that anybody, except perhaps his family, knew his real name, and they got so used to calling him Santa that they sometimes had to stop and think.

Leroy Sholtz was a naturally heavyset man who turned prematurely white haired. He grew a beard, also white, and let his thick, white hair grow long. He was a physical natural for the part of Santa Claus. He was also in the right place at the right time. Working in Bethlehem, Pennsylvania, known as Christmas City, USA, he began working part time between Thanksgiving and Christmas Eve as Santa Claus at

Orr's Department store on Main Street. He had a pat on the head and a kiss on the cheek for every little kid who sat on his knee, believing in him. For the mischievous ones who doubted his integrity, he had a surprise and a "Ho-ho-ho" when they tugged on his beard.

Soon, Leroy understood that this was God's calling for him. He changed his legal name to Santa C. Claus in 1980. He told friends that he did this so that when children asked him if he was really Santa Claus, he could answer truthfully. He surely knew God's purpose when he was accepted as the resident Santa Claus at the North Pole, a tourist attraction in the Adirondack Mountains of Upstate New York. He and his wife disappeared from Bethlehem for many years.

Familiar with the unforgettable letter, written in 1897 to Virginia O'Hanlon by Francis Church of the *New York Sun*, I certainly understood the spirit of Santa Claus, but in my child's heart, as we are all children at heart, I always believed in him and knew—well, hoped—that one day, I would meet the real Santa Claus.

I was thirty-eight years old at the time. He first appeared as an apparition in the lens of my video camera. It was 1984, and Bethlehem, Pennsylvania, was giving birth to a new savior. The great factory known to all the locals simply as "Steel" was letting employees go, closing major sections of the once nearly seventeen-mile-long industrial plant.

When we first moved back to the Lehigh Valley, I made a little extra cash doing consumer product surveys. Always warm and welcoming people, all sixty-seven ethnic groups of them, many of Bethlehem's citizens invited me into their homes for coffee and whatever delicious, homemade pastry they had to offer. In return for their hospitality and cooperation, I had to listen to sad stories filled with worry about, "What to do now?" "Steel" was always their lives. Grandpa, dad, husband, son, mother, daughter, all were a part of the history of Bethlehem Steel.

A young lawyer, Jeffrey Parks, had a vision for the stricken Bethlehem but no money. Yet local folks knew that in a city named for Christ's birthplace, miracles could happen. Parks talked to my husband, who was born and raised in Bethlehem and was back in town and newly working as director of marketing for First National Bank. It took three rejections by his boss, but finally, at my husband's insistence that he would "bank" his job on it, the seed money was provided by the bank, and Musikfest was born in Bethlehem.

It was a fledgling enterprise, this nine-day music festival steeped in German heritage. It promised over six-hundred free musical performances, scattered around nine different performance venues throughout the downtown area, and everyone prayed it could keep its promises. Everything used was obtained cheaply or for free. Bethlehem suddenly became a city of volunteer workers! I was one of them, videotaping all the festivities for posterity and promotion at all the sites as fast as I could run from "*platz* to *platz*," that is, performance place to performance place.

It was Volksplatz (the people's place) where I first saw him. It was just a passing glance of a jolly-looking man, dressed in a lightweight summer shirt. When I zoomed in, I noticed that his shirt had a reindeer pattern on it.

He was only a face in the crowd, but I saw him again later that day at Leiderplatz, the place of song, enjoying a hot dog and cold soda, and then again in the evening at Festplatz, under the great expanse of the Fahy Bridge, doing the "chicken dance" with some little children. As a matter of fact, for the next two days, he kept popping up in my lens, one day wearing a shirt with an elf motif, the next day one with holly. I mentioned his unusual dress and appearance to my husband on our way home late one night.

"Oh yes," he said. "That's Santa Claus."

"Yeah, honey," I said. "I think you're working too hard."

"No seriously, that's him, the real Santa Claus. He's trying to get some work with the festival."

And he did. The last day of the first Musikfest in 1984, a particularly hot August day, I stopped back at Press Platz, or what I liked to call "the command post," to replenish my film supply (I was taking still pictures too). Santa was there, hoping for a ride back to his hotel to get his red suit. He was going to lead the closing parade! Before I could speak, and because I had all the proper stickers and passes to get through the crowds, I was volunteered to deliver Santa Claus to Main Street, fully dressed and ready to go in two hours!

Santa's hotel was almost forty minutes away. Out and back again left us little time, and my baby blue Volkswagen bug's top speed was fifty-five. I decided we'd take Route 22, the fastest way to Easton, and also the busiest. It was very late in the afternoon. The trip out would be okay, but we risked heavy commuter traffic on the return. Santa, being a talkative man, provided much of his life's story before we were halfway to our destination.

Indeed a jolly man, after his wife's death, he lost heart in his job and got himself into a little trouble with the North Pole. He told me, "…it had something to do with wine and women," and then he "ho-ho-ho'd," shaking all over, and winked at me between wheezes. Santa, by then, was not a healthy man. His heart condition had become quite serious.

We arrived in record time since "Herbie," as my kids called the bug, had never run so well. I wondered if indeed the man had some sort of magic influence. It must have been around five o'clock when we entered his room and hurriedly prepared. I filled his sack with "a few small things for the kids" while he went into the bathroom to put on "the suit." I wondered, in a perverse way, *What would people think if they knew I was in a motel room with Santa Claus?*

In a few minutes, Santa emerged from the bathroom in all his red and white velvet glory, wheezing. He quickly swallowed a nitroglycerin pill with a glass of very cold water. Away we went back to Route 22 in the heat, at the going-home hour, a woman driving a baby blue Volkswagen with the windows down and a white-bearded man in a red suit, long white hair blowing in the wind, looking very much like Santa Claus! I imagined all the homecoming conversations:

"Hey, honey. Hey, kids. Guess who passed me on Route 22?"

"Hey, everybody, you'll never believe what I saw on Route 22."

"You're gonna think I'm crazy, but…"

"Listen up, family, you're going to love this."

On our way back, I learned a great deal more about the real Santa Claus. Not a saint, to be sure, but a wonderful, warm, generous human being who loved children, people, and life. I came to think he was more wonderful than the imaginary Santa. He spoke of God as a close friend. He said, "Mrs. Santa, now there was a saint for putting up with the likes of me. Ho-ho-ho."

It was the last I was to see of Santa. After Musikfest, he drifted on to other places. A few years later, I was reading the morning newspaper. It's something I rarely have time to do, much less have time to look at the obituaries. There he was, saying good-bye to me. The article did him justice. It mentioned that he tried to buy a cemetery plot near his home in the Adirondacks, presumably to be close to Mrs. Santa. Because of criticism by local business people that it would be bad taste to have a tombstone reading, "Santa Claus," which young children might see, he decided instead to be buried in Colorado. The article said that his stone was simply engraved, "A Child of God."

I have been troubled lately, sometimes feeling deeply disappointed by friends and family, and feeling very sorry for myself. While looking through some old photo albums, the obituary reading "Santa C. Claus's Ashes to Be Buried on Colorado Plains," dropped out of the pages. My first thought in that present mood was, "Oh God, even Santa Claus is dead!" It's a wide and fragile bridge between self-pity and self-sacrifice that can only be crossed when guided by a great soul, perhaps a saint, who leads the way.

I read the article from *The Morning Call* again and studied the picture. It revealed an intense man with happy, wise eyes peering over a pair of spectacles. He seemed to be saying, "No, honey, I'm most certainly not dead. Ho-ho-ho."

It says his heart "gave out" at age fifty-nine. Well, reporters don't always get the context right. We all know that Santa's heart gives out eternally. That funny, "wheezingly" wonderful man lives in my heart. Yes, Santa lives forever, and Santa is forever real for me and, hopefully, for all who read or hear this. Because, you see, we are all of us, like Leroy Sholtz, simply, "A Child of God."

MY MYSTERIOUS STRANGER

I suppose by most people's standards, it was an odd relationship. It even started out oddly. You could perhaps call it a blind date in a way. I certainly walked into it blindly, having little or no idea what I was getting into. Sometimes a third party intervenes, and you feel this pressure to say, "Okay, okay, yes, I'll try this," just to get him off your back. I was willing and ready enough to admit my need and dependence on the third party, so it seemed like it was on an impulse to agree to "work with" Sam and "see what happens." I spent the rest of my life learning the power and purpose of impulse.

Right from the beginning, our relationship took on a very private, intimate tone. We met in quiet, secluded places, which mostly, but not always, excluded others from our intercourse. Mostly, it was libraries. It wasn't just that he was so much older than I was; we quickly established a kind of spiritual equality that dismissed that issue, and it was more a certain "delicacy" in learning to handle one another's lives and souls that caused us such temerity. We knew at once that this was right, "meant to be" as the Romantics would say. He hated that stuff, I was to learn. Yet it was difficult at first to begin our relationship. I was afraid to fail, and he could not be sure of me. Would I get it right? Was I wasting his and my time? Would I understand? What was my ultimate purpose? Was I just a foolish, romantic young girl?

In the beginning, I had to report back to my third party with "progress reports" on how it was going. I found myself lying a lot, an aspect of character of which I was not and am not proud, but the inquiry did get in the way of what was happening between Sam and me. It's hardly that this stuff was so private; I mean it was like the world knew about his life, but the world did not and could not and should not know about how his life and my life happened to come together. Call it selfish, but when we were together, I always felt like he was talking to just me, like we had some "special" connection. I believe he felt it too, which was the whole purpose of meeting and connecting with me. My Sam just needed a real friend, maybe even a secret friend, to whom he could talk, share secrets, and try to be understood. Despite my initial fear, ignorance, and insecurity, I really, desperately needed and wanted to be that friend. And he desperately needed and wanted a reporter to finally get it right, not just the facts, but more importantly, the feelings.

The intimacy came in slow stages, and I'm not talking about sex here. That whole idea is so incredibly absurd, although, in another time and other circumstances I could not imagine myself being able to resist him, coming to know Sam as I eventually did. Even in his age, I found him incredibly sexy and imagined what he was like in his prime with that wildly thick hair, full moustache, and penetrating eyes. He had a long Aryan nose that sloped into a slight hook, which, I think, made his moustache look like he was always smiling. But, it was a sardonic smile with the slightest, almost unnoticeable twist to the left side. Most people didn't notice this about him, but I loved it. Oh, I loved it! I sometimes wished I *were* born sooner. There was such a fire in my Sammy!

He was not a particularly big man, yet he seemed that way because of his spirit, energy, and intensity. Sam was, if nothing else, *intense*. We started out like most strangers first meeting each other. We talked about where we came from, what our interests were, what sign we were born under, the latter being important to him, surprisingly. Little by little, as a cat lover draws a wild cat toward him, eventually with food and gentle stroking, Sam and I stretched beyond the short answer version of these essential questions. By the way, Sam adored cats, viewed them as superior beings—well, at least superior to humans. Mostly, Sam had a great deal of disdain for the human race, but I knew that was just words. Rarely do you find a man with so much love in him.

Sam was born in a small Midwestern town of strict Presbyterian parents; I immediately started comparing the impact of his childhood experiences with my small-town, Upstate New York, altogether-too-Catholic upbringing. I rebelled and tried to escape in college. I wondered how his defiant spirit dealt with this problem in the context of his life and time. It didn't take very long for us to meet and commune on this issue, rebels that we both were. I remember confessing to him at one point when he was particularly willing to make himself vulnerable to me. "Sam," I said, "When I was drowning, all I remember before 'going over' was saying to myself, 'This is it, and it's okay. It's not the way they taught me. It's not the way they said it would be.'" He really seemed to like that. Maybe that opened a lot more doors for me.

Sam was married only once, so was I. He was absolutely devoted to his wife and their children, until he lost most of them: first, his baby son, then his favorite daughter, then his wife. His other two daughters became alienated from him. I've been alienated too, but I never lost my family, not totally. It seems to me there's only so much grief a man, no matter how strong, can bear, but Sam's unconquerable spirit kept him going somehow. He said it was his sense of humor, explaining to me that the core of all humor was sadness. In my irresistible passion for him, I believed it was his genius, a gift, an amazing something a few distinct, special souls bring into the world. He was blessed, or perhaps, damned with such a gift. All along, I knew he was teaching me, even as he taught so many before me, but I swear, so much of what he said was a mystery to me at the time. Perhaps, it *was* his sadness that drew me to him, even as much as his marvelous humor.

Yet there was more. My probing eventually led us into conversations about the meaning of life and humankind's relationship with God. At the time that we first met, each of us had arrived at some of the same "bizarre" conclusions. We had similar "dreams," precognitive warnings, communications with disembodied souls. Sam revealed to me that he was born with a "veil over his face." I remember my grandmother telling me about such people. "It" simply "wasn't the way that we were taught." This singular aspect was probably the strongest bond between us. From this point on, he absolutely owned me, and I had all but disconnected with the third party who brought us together but no longer seemed to exist. Now, screw the worldly stuff! Sam and I were on a spiritual quest together.

All the other fascinating aspects of Sam's life, and the boring, or so I thought, aspects of my life, came together. His destitute beginnings, my poverty and drunken father; his adventurous youth and my desperate attempts to find myself, even to volunteer for war; his amazing accomplishments, my under-rated achievements; all these things came together and exploded into our relationship, and there we were. We both understood. This was the reason we met. We weren't just a famous writer and an ambitious reporter; we were two human beings, two hungry souls, needing one another in order to understand the mystery of life.

Despite all of his remarkable accomplishments, Sam knew that time was running out, and he had not yet achieved what he hoped would be his final statement of truth. This was important to him, indescribably important. He felt himself a mysterious stranger in a world, if not quite ready to hear and understand him, perhaps even totally hostile to his version of the truth. I told him he was a Christ figure in this respect. He just laughed at me and said, "Christ couldn't tell a joke as well as I can," and he took precautions to protect his thought.

Few in the world, in either his generation or mine, including his own daughters, knew of his despair. As with so many of genius gift, they have too much insight, too much light in a world so dark with ignorance, intolerance, greed, power lust, and insecurity about their purpose. Christ could make it clear in simple parables; Sam could try to make it clear in humor. Each would ask God for a way out.

When you love someone who thinks about suicide, as I did, you beat yourself up wondering what you could have said or done that might have comforted, changed; you wish you could have been there, as if that would help. Sam didn't understand, then, how much I loved and understood him. How could he? He only knew his isolation. Thank God, something in him compelled him not to pull the trigger and end it all. Always and forever, he was a courageous and curious man. I guess, after all, he wondered what might happen if he just held out.

What happened was nothing short of amazing. He taught me the power of creation, and I stood in absolute awe. Until now, I had never really appreciated what it is that an author does, and a humorous aside, if you'll permit me. Sam said I should calm down and take time for humorous asides. I learned from him that men can, in fact, experience the pain of birthing a child. He birthed a most amazing child and must have felt as overwhelmed and amazed as Saint Elizabeth, the old-aged mother of John the Baptist. He confirmed for me the simple, elemental truth that, so long as you live, you have something to give. Nevertheless, it was not an easy child with whom to live.

This child was set above the human race, seeing us with all our warts. This child asked questions for which we, in our ignorance, have no answers. Parents hate that! You know, stuff like, "Why do we continue to do things this way if we know they don't work?" This incredible and oftentimes overbearing child even pointed out how ridiculous and inferior our sexuality was! I thought Sam particularly brave in this, remembering the taboos and double standards of my own upbringing, which paled to his Victorian standards! I remember making my mother crazy when I was in college, telling her that I wish I had been raised by the Onondaga Indians instead of mixed-up Catholics. I would have had fewer hang-ups. Sam was subtly proud of his familial relations with Native Americans. It wasn't until many years later that I learned from a cousin at a family funeral that Sam's family and mine were related, however distant, by Native American ancestors. By this time I was not surprised, only intrigued.

I guess Sam's relation with his last child, whom he called "The Mysterious Stranger," was a classic love-hate thing. I do know that he feared what he had brought forth. Creating new life is the riskiest thing that we creatures on earth can do. You just never know where this kid is going or what it's going to do! The thing is, once out of you, it has a life of its own, whether it is born of the womb or born of the brain; it makes no difference. In the end, Sam tried to put the genie back into the bottle. I guess he feared the unknown as much as the rest of us, and being the good parent that he tried to be, he was worried about what this child might do to the others.

Looking back, I realize that I probably had just enough time with my dear, dear Sam to accomplish what we both had set for ourselves in this life. At the time, however, I wanted to rave and wail at my deprivation. How could this come to an end? Why did I have to leave? There's so much more! I need him! He needs me!

But the third party came back with deadlines and requirements, demanding a finale. I don't even remember saying good-bye to Sam, because I don't think we ever did say good-bye. We grew together; we crossed a bridge between time and space and met each other simply as human beings. Together we learned that there are no good-byes, only deadlines. So, I turned in my paper, and I got a degree, and oh so very much more that I could never have foreseen when first I said, "Okay, okay."

Sam will always be with me. He's with me oftentimes in my dreams. He's with me when I teach my students and when I share with my family. My own children are well acquainted with him and his family. We even went together, to visit his home where they learned how he tore the telephone off the wall and shot his typewriter! They loved him all the more for that. I love him forever! I thank God for him, and for my chance to get to know him. He has so enriched my life; I can only hope I did so for him.

I would say, "Thank you, Sam, for sharing your life, your work, and your soul with me, mine, and all of mankind. Thank you for your redeeming humor, your painfully probing mind, your self-sacrifice to see it through when you really wanted out. I still, and always will, see you as a bit of a Christ figure. I love you my dear friend, Sam, Mr. Clemens, the inimitable, incomparable Mark Twain!

THE CHRISTMAS RING

Some people used to say that my grandmother, Rhoda, was a strange and loose lady. That's what the self-appointed "good" Christians would say. Mostly I ignored them because, to me, she was a wonderful, fascinating lady. In so many ways, I wanted to grow up to be like her. I adored her, still do, but I suppose she did have some funny ways about her, or so it seemed when I was young. Even so, those things made me laugh, like the funny way she pronounced some words. "Man" was "Min" for example and "alulinum" for "aluminum," but my favorite was "tay" for "tea." And some of her ways had a strange effect on me. She never allowed us kids to call each other "stupid" or "idiot." She warned, "If you call another person something bad or sad, it will come back to you." I don't know how she did it, but she had me believing that if I called my little brother a pig, then I would become a pig, at least until I said I was sorry and meant it. She had a certain soft power over us.

Gramma Rhoda's parents came from a small town in England called Great Wishford in Wiltshire, "not far from Stonehenge," she would constantly remind me. I had no idea what Stonehenge was until I was in high school; nevertheless, I was impressed. Among the many things she told me that people in Great Wishford believed, like most English people, was that no matter what ails you "a good cup of tay" will fix it, as if by magic. I drank a lot of tea as a youth, usually only Lipton. Gramma insisted that it was 100 percent natural and 100 percent real, but she loved their slogan that "Lipton's gets into more hot water than anything." She thought that was so funny, and it always made her laugh. I think now that she related to "getting into hot water."

It was the fifties, and since my mother worked, I spent a lot of growing up time with my grandmother;

consequently, I became a Lipton fan as well. We drank hot tea in the winter and Lipton iced tea in the summer. It never occurred to me that my grandmother loved this tea because it was inexpensive. Today, I'm still a great tea drinker, but I can afford exotic teas and often drink them, but when I'm in trouble, I always turn to Lipton.

Rhoda means "Rose," which in the Western world is the symbol of love. According to Greek mythology, it symbolizes immortal love or a union that will never fade, even through time or death. To the Romans it meant a symbolic carrier of secrets or a tacit understanding. When I studied Latin in high school, I learned that when the Romans hung roses at their meeting places, it meant that nothing that was said or done there was to be repeated, hence the phrase "sub rosa" or "under the roses." I always thought the name fit her perfectly, and I am proud to bear it as my middle name and my mother's as my first, Bernice, "a bringer of victory."

I don't know if my grandmother knew that when she named her daughter, as Rhoda was not privileged with very much education. In her generation she was lucky to get through the eighth grade. She may have intuitively known it, however, as my grandmother was the most intuitive person I have ever known. Because she was so victimized in her own young life, surely she wanted her daughter to be victorious. Sometimes we take names for granted, having all kinds of reasons for naming a child, as in my immediate family every child had to be named for someone previous in the family. Personally, I like the way Native Americans name their children; it allows for so much individuality, but we descendents of the Europeans are stuck with our customs for good or ill.

Speaking of intuition, even as a child I dreamed about one day having a daughter, and I named my favorite dolly "Veronica." I loved the name before I knew the biblical story of Veronica, a story to which this day brings tears to my eyes, a woman so helpless yet moved to such compassion, offered the only thing that she had to the suffering Jesus, who so appreciated and acknowledged her gift that He left the lasting impression of his face on her veil. I would not understand until many years and many journeys later about all the connections in life. I did not get to name my daughter Veronica because I had to make compromises. Had my grandmother lived that long, she would have given me the reason…and the courage. Without knowing what I now know, she would have intuited that Veronica shares a common root in the Greek with Bernice.

My grandmother never worried much about money. She had little of it, but she always said, "I have all I need, and if I want more, I can wish for it." This always mystified me. She lived in a big, old Victorian house that had once been the pride of a renowned local judge. That was in the nineteenth century, but in the twentieth century, the neighborhood deteriorated into borderline slums. So as a child, I was privileged to live in the great divide between two very different worlds. My grandmother's Victorian mansion-slash-slum house was a splendid example of the opulence of the era in 1870 when it was first built. It had a huge front porch that my grandmother and I sat on in the summertime as she would teach me the lyrics of every song from "A Bicycle Built for Two" to "The White Cliffs of Dover" to "San Francisco," but she only liked the Tony Bennett version. Also, anything by Frank Sinatra was cool with her. I still know all these lyrics, but I could never sing like my Gramma Rhoda. She had a beautiful, crystalline second soprano voice, which she thankfully passed down to my daughter, who sadly, does not know the lyrics.

How that voice still rings in my ears! How I remember it rising above the katydids' songs, floating over the humid summer air like the perfume of summer blossoms. We'd have iced tea on that porch and then pass through the anteroom lined with four beveled glass windows, about two-by-six, two on each side of the huge, oak door. The door was so heavy that I could not open it myself until I was ten years old. Inside there was a coat rack on each wall, a vase to hold umbrellas, and a box in which to deposit your "rubbers." I couldn't get my grandmother to stop calling "goulashes" by the term "rubbers," even when I was a teenager and deeply embarrassed by the term.

Next there was another door, a dark mahogany with two beautiful stained glass windows, three-by-six, one on each side, delicately designed into abstract floral patterns and stained in soft shades of yellows, orange, and bronze, which allowed the morning light to pour into what seemed to me the huge, castle-like hallway. My childhood fantasy ran away with me whenever I entered that hallway. I was a fairy princess entering the magical crystal cave, or later when I was a teenager, I became the young Elizabeth about to enter the coronation hall. It seemed to me a vast space of endless dreams and possibilities. On the left was an amazing stained glass window beside the winding staircase. It was a garden scene lush with color: purples, greens, brown, and soft rose, framed in a glistening mahogany staircase. The window spread eight feet across, rose twelve feet high, and ruled the foyer. How I loved to watch the diffused light dance around the walls and the old oak floors! Gramma said it was her version of the "stairway to heaven," but it wasn't really heaven—it was only the bedrooms.

At the base of the stairs, the banister on which I often slid down, was a small reception room in which guests of the nineteenth century waited to be announced. It was a cozy area with built in benches covered in crimson velvet cushions. In the 1950s it was a hospital for a little girl's sick dollies, or Rapunzel's tower, where I remained trapped for hours. Sometimes it would be my fort where I sought refuge from my younger Apache brother's warrior attacks. Directly across from the great mahogany door was the access to what had been the grand dining room with its own fireplace and a butler's pantry at the end. As a girl child, I envisioned finely dressed royal duchesses with feathers in their hair dining in that room and a stiff old butler coming out of the swinging door every time a little bell was rung, bidding him to serve some new and wonderfully delicious delicacy.

In reality, Gramma had turned it into an efficiency apartment, bedroom-slash-living room by the fireplace, dining area near the butler's pantry, which was now a narrow little kitchen, complete with stove and refrigerator. The woman who lived there for all the years that I could remember had been a fairly successful opera singer whom my grandmother said "married" the wrong man. Actually, I came to understand that he was already married, but my grandmother wanted to spare me the explanation. Lavinia Whittington was a stately lady in spite of her reduced station in life when I knew her. She liked to wear makeup and was always well dressed. Sometimes she wore false hair, the same shade as mine. She had no living relatives and left no will. After she died, sleeping in a big Queen Anne chair my grandmother had bought at the "junque" store, my grandmother found those beautiful hairpieces and gave them to me. "It would make Vinnie happy," she said, "and they will bring you music when you wear them."

Gramma, my mother, my brother, and I, and the funeral director, were the only people at her service. Afterward my mother and grandmother went through Lavinia's few things. What we didn't want or Gramma couldn't use we gave to the Salvation Army. My mother loved "the Army" because they ministered to "the world's most rejected souls."

My grandmother told me only to wear those hairpieces for very special occasions, and I heeded her words. I only wore them on the special occasions that called for me to pile and pin my long hair on the top of my head. When I did, I always heard the music. I got my first kiss and later my first proposal while wearing those hairpieces. I wore them on my wedding day. Years later, I gave them to my daughter, who has the same color hair.

To the right of the grand hallway was a set of double doors, which opened into Gramma's double parlor. In 1870 the TV living room had been the gentlemen's parlor, separated by heavy oak double sliding doors which led to Gramma's bedroom, formerly the ladies' drawing room. The gentleman's parlor still smelled of smoke because my grandmother's longtime boyfriend was a cigar smoker and spent his evening hours in that room watching *The Ed Sullivan Show, The Red Skelton Show,* and *I Love Lucy.* I remember her opening and closing those doors when she wanted to get dressed. My Gramma Rhoda always smelled of Pond's cold cream and rose water, and her bedroom-slash-the ladies' drawing room exuded those sweet, subtle aromas. Even now, when I clean my face with Pond's cold cream, as my gramma taught me, I feel loved.

But the kitchen was my favorite place, especially during Advent, when it was filled with the smell of cinnamon, chocolate, and mulling spices. My grandmother, mother, and I always had our "tay" while we were cooking and baking, but it was mostly the smells that warmed us as we watched the snow fill up my gramma's big backyard and obscure the old carriage house, which then held six of her tenants' cars: two Fords, two Chevys, one Pontiac, and one Edsel.

One Ford belonged to a young student of the ministry; the other Ford belonged to an elderly couple, Eloise and Frank Strauss, who lived on the third floor and often took twenty minutes to climb the stairs; they never had children, and only the husband could read. He was a bank clerk, and she worked as a short-order cook in a popular diner. One Chevy belonged to Shirley

Little, my childhood favorite tenant, a young woman from what we called "the North Country," trying to help her family. "The North Country" was desperately poor farm land in the northern part of Upstate New York, cold, forbidding, often rocky, land. Unfortunately, Shirley's Chevy was a lemon, and it mostly stayed in the carriage house because she couldn't afford to fix it. The other Chevy belonged to a young college student at Syracuse University, whom we rarely saw but he often complained about his father, who paid his rent. The Pontiac belonged to a tired middle-aged man who was a lawyer but rarely ever had a case. Gramma said he had been raised "with a silver spoon in his mouth," but his family lost everything in the stock market crash. The Edsel belonged to my grandmother's best friend in the world. Scotty had been born into a very wealthy family but was abused as a little boy by the family's hostler. Scotty never told his family, but he did become depressed and sometimes acted out, becoming an embarrassment to his prestigious family. I don't remember that Gramma ever told me how they met. I just know that they were like brother and sister. My grandmother gave him a home and a family, and he adored her for it the rest of his life.

My grandmother's house had a beautiful backyard filled with trees and flowers. The neighborhood kids and I could play Tarzan or cool off on a summer day with the big pitchers of Kool-Aid Rhoda would bring us, along with the best peanut butter and jelly sandwiches on earth. But that came to an abrupt end after what happened one day. Sally Mae lived alone with her mother in one of the apartment buildings on the block, which had replaced a grand old Victorian that fell into neglect. At age seven, Sally Mae was the very first African American girl I ever got close to. We used to touch each other's skin to see if it felt any different, and our hair; that *did* feel different. I loved Sally Mae; she made me giggle all the time, but one day while we were enjoying our peanut butter sandwiches under the big trees, Sally Mae's eyes went real funny and seemed to roll back in her head. She fell down to the ground and started shaking violently, like she was doing some kind of jig, but only lying down. I ran to my grandmother while the other children stood around horrified and mesmerized. My grandmother grabbed a dishcloth, rolled it, and ran out to Sally Mae, who was writhing on the ground. Gramma rammed the dishcloth into Sally Mae's mouth and told us children to make sure it stayed there while she ran to call an ambulance. We were all so frightened, and the ambulance seemed to take forever. I kept talking to Sally Mae, even though I was crying, but I don't think she heard me. I never saw her again, and my gramma said she thought that Sally Mae and her mother moved away. I overheard my grandmother telling my mother that even though epilepsy was better understood, it still carried a stigma. At the time I had no idea what a stigma was, but I have since had ample opportunity to learn. After that the neighborhood children rarely came around, and I didn't really want to play in the yard anymore.

I mostly stayed indoors with my gramma and "helped" her clean all the "light housekeeping" rooms that she rented out to life's less fortunate. At seven or eight, I wasn't much help, but I was ever fascinated with those grand rooms, now with their little hot plate burners and shared bathroom privileges. Each room had a different-colored marble fireplace topped with richly carved mantles. My favorite was the pink one, which once might have been a daughter's bedroom. And then there was the brown one, which reminded me of vanilla ice cream with chocolate swirls in it. It had a grand mantle with tiny, delicately carved cherubs at each end. At one end of that room there had been a "dumb waiter," which my grandmother had sealed. "I ain't never gonna be no dumb waiter!" she exclaimed. My guess was that room had once been the master suite.

The servants' quarters on the third floor were the most fascinating to me. Gramma rented these rooms out pretty cheap, mostly to young people who had moved down from "the North Country" where there was no work and no opportunity, people like Shirley Little, about nineteen, who got a job as a secretary at a roofing company and sent half of her salary home to help with the five remaining brothers and sisters. She used to let me dress up in her clothes, and she took pictures of me with her Brownie camera. She said I reminded her of her little sister, Sarah.

I had free range of the third floor except to help Gramma carry the mop, broom, and dustpan down the back stairs, which emptied into that fabulous kitchen with the big, black wrought-iron stove. When I was ten, she let me load the coal into the stove, but only if she watched me do it. How I loved that old house! It seemed to wrap around me. It offered me comfort, excitement, adventure, education, solace. It never occurred to me that it was a borderline slum house, a place to be ashamed of, a last refuge for the desperate. To me, back then, it was paradise on earth. Being with my grandmother in that place, at that time, was heaven to me.

One Christmas season, after completing the chores and stoking the stove, my grandmother and I sat down for our "tay." She did what was to me a most mysterious thing. "It's time," she whispered in my ear while holding her forefinger to her lips. Perhaps because I had just become a teenager, and I was menstruating, my grandmother figured I was a young woman now, as she had been. "It's time for you to learn about the ring."

It was the first day of Advent, which meant that my parents would be making me go to boring old church for some reason that I did not understand. What I think I liked most about my grandmother was that she never made me do anything. "You don't have to do it," she teased, "but then you'll never know the magic in it." I always wanted to find the magic, and when I didn't, she told me I wasn't trying hard enough. I sometimes thought that since she was Protestant, only Protestants could feel the magic. She told me that wasn't so. "It works for everyone," she insisted, "even the Jews!" My grandmother's parents were Jewish, but when Rhoda's mother died delivering her eighth baby, her father denounced his faith and a few months later married a Gentile much younger than he. My gramma said, "That woman was the original wicked stepmother."

"What ring?" I asked her.

"The Christmas ring," she replied.

"The Christmas ring?"

"I keep it tucked away in a special place and usually only bring it out at Christmas time, the way my mother would have brought such a precious thing out to be shared only during Hanukah," Gramma explained.

"What's Hanukah?" I asked.

"It's a special time when people remember the things that are most important to them like loving, and forgiving, and being grateful for their blessings."

I was young, but I understood and felt what my grandmother was saying. Years later I would appreciate the faith, courage, and sacrifice these holidays represented, and it didn't matter whether you called yourself Jewish, Catholic, Protestant, Islam, Hindu, Buddhist, or whatever. It wasn't about aligning yourself with one group or another; it was about being human, knowing that we are all one in the eyes of God, whatever we may call Him, or Her. This was all pretty heavy stuff to be laid upon a teenager whose major focus was upon her skin problems.

I knew something wonderful was about to happen; the tea was brewing, and Gramma closed the sliding doors between the parlors. Then she pulled out the bottom drawer of her Empire-style chest of drawers. She reached past her perfectly folded panties, teddies, and corsets, which in the fifties were filled with steel stays instead of whalebone.

"I keep it in red," she said, "because red is the color of life, and there is so much life in this little sack." I felt a tingle in my body and unconsciously looked around to see if anyone was watching us. I felt a little dizzy from the scent of roses that emanated from that drawer. My heart was skipping beats.

"I wanted to give this to your mother so that she could give it to you, but there is a wall between your mother and me that would not allow it." At thirteen, one is so eager to gobble up all that one can about the mystery of life. The greater mystery, I now know, is why my grandmother decided at this point to tell me about the wall. Surely she knew me better than I knew myself.

"Your mother was my fourth child," Gramma explained. Your uncle Merrill was my third. They were the survivors. I married very young and very foolishly. Your grandfather and I lived in great poverty. We had no heat in the winter, and my beautiful twins, Rhoda Mae and Bessie, died in their second year." She told me this story in a monotone, as if she had lived through it and told it a hundred times. I was mesmerized as I listened to her.

She carried the little red sack out to the kitchen, and I followed in a trance. She placed it ceremoniously on the old Formica table, which stood in front of the iron stove and poured us each a cup of Lipton tea. She took honey; I took milk and sugar.

"Grandpa and I had too many differences and too many heartbreaks to stay together." We sat silently for a while, sipping our "tay" and watching big, downy flakes of snow pile up on her kitchen windowsill. There was a nice warm fire going in the old iron stove; the tenants were all upstairs doing what they did in the evening hours behind closed doors. Frank Strauss was surely reading the newspaper to Eloise, Shirley

Little was writing home and preparing a check to be sent in her letter, the college student was studying, and Joel was reviewing the case of a possible client.

"We had a terrible fight," my grandmother recalled. "I remember throwing dishes at your grandfather and then running out of the house. I was so angry and hurt I did not think of your mother and uncle at that moment. All I could think was where to run, and I ran to your aunt Lillian. I could not imagine in that moment that I would lose my children, but I did. Grandpa took them to his mistress's house."

I was thirteen; I'm not sure that I knew exactly what a mistress was, but I was beginning to feel a little overwhelmed by my grandmother's tale. "Why is she telling me all of this now?" I wished I were six or seven again, sliding down the banister in the great anteroom of Gramma's house.

In the ensuing hour, I learned that my mother and uncle were taken by my grandfather and his mistress, and my grandmother, "declared an unfit mother" had no access to her children. When she tried to bring them presents at Christmastime, she was chased away with a shotgun. All this time my mother believed as she was told, that her mother had abandoned her and her brother.

"It was during the Great Depression, something maybe you have learned about in school?" Gramma asked. "My sister, Lil, owned a small nursery, and I stayed with her, as did my two brothers and their wives. We all worked the farm and the nursery, and that's how we got through those tough times. We had just enough for ourselves, but we had lots of fun times singing and playing cards, but always, always, my heart was aching for my lost children, especially because there was my niece and nephew always romping around."

I had never seen my grandmother cry before this moment, so I was speechless and paralyzed when I saw the tear roll down her cheek. She wiped it quickly with her ever-present laced-lined hanky, which she kept tucked in her bra. I pretended that I didn't see. In the background I could hear one of the tenants letting himself in through the great mahogany door and the muffled sounds of rock and roll coming from Shirley Little's distant radio.

"My sister and I were very close, and she knew that I loved jewelry, nice jewelry, which I could never afford." I noted that even now, Rhoda didn't have much jewelry, but what she did have was very nice. My grandmother was a very "classy chick."

"It was Christmastime," she continued, "and in spite of everything, it had been a pretty good year for us. Heh," she shrugged, "a lot of funerals, I think." Gramma got up to stoke the stove. As she lifted the heavy, wrought-iron lid, with this strange instrument she called a "lid lifter," I jumped up to get the coal from the bucket, which sat beside the stove. With the fire replenished and more hot water poured into the beautiful Wedgewood teapot she always used, we sat back down across from one another at the old second-hand kitchen table with chairs that did not match, all which she got from the local secondhand dealer. To this day I haunt such places looking for treasure, and when I find something, nothing makes me happier.

It seemed to me that there was a glistening in my grandmother's eyes as she spoke. "I was absolutely flabbergasted when I opened it Christmas morning. I had never seen anything so beautiful, and my sister gave it to me. It didn't matter one iota that she got it at a pawn shop." At this point I was so anxious to see what was inside, I felt that I could scream.

"Are you ready, honey?" she asked.

Was I ready? I was going to faint if she didn't open that sack at that moment. A small woman, only five-foot-two, Gramma had tiny hands with beautiful nails, which she "buffed" every day and only painted for special occasions. I watched with awe as those tiny fingers tenderly tore at the strings of the sack.

"Close your eyes and put your hands out," she commanded. I felt the little bump and a sudden, slight sensation of heat as the ring landed in my hands, face down. "Now open your eyes."

I was amazed, out of breath, eyes wide as I looked upon the most beautiful ring I had ever seen. My grandmother leaned back in her chair, arms folded, a soft smile on her lips as she let me study the ring. In many ways it seemed indescribable, so unique was this ring. It sat upon a band of white gold. It was a large stone, about the size of one of the red-skinned peanuts my grandmother always had laying in a bowl in the living room. All around its circumference were tiny white diamonds. As I held it in my fingers, it felt very warm, and even soft, but the most exciting thing was its color, or I should say, colors.

As I turned it in the light, it shimmered a rainbow of colors that seemed to vibrate. Starring at it, I thought how whimsical it was. I felt like I was chasing light. I felt giddy and giggled. My grandmother giggled back at me.

"It's magical, you know," she whispered.

"Yes, it is," I responded.

"No, seriously, baby." Her tone completely changed. "This ring is magical."

Now she had me a little nervous. I knew that my great grandmother had been a fortuneteller. I knew both my mother and grandmother had precognitive dreams. I was suddenly reminded of some of the strange feelings and thoughts that I was afraid to share with anyone. What was she talking about? What should I do with this ring?

"Of course, the first thing I did when I opened it was to put it on my finger and kiss and hug my sister. When I let my niece and nephew look at it, I felt a sudden and deep yearning for my own children. I subconsciously turned the ring into my palm, squeezed my hand shut, held it over my heart, closed my eyes, and wished for my babies to be with me." As she told me this, she mimicked the motion I should make.

"It was nineteen thirty-three. Many would say one of the worst years of the Depression. And it was a terrible winter." As she sipped her tea and I played with the ring, she told me how she and her family struggled, but managed; how frugal they were, how they reused everything, wasted nothing, and even managed to save a little. She described how wonderful dinnertime was around her sister's table, and while it was simple food, there was always plenty of it. She said the women did the dishes and sang along while the men played their guitars, and how they all went to bed early because they worked so hard and were so tired.

"It happened on the Epiphany," she mused. "The postman had a hard time getting down our long drive in the snow. Those old cars, you know, weren't very good in the snow." She told me when she saw the return address on the letter, she sank to her knees. Her sister helped her up, sat her at a chair at the kitchen table, and told her not to open it until she made some tea. My grandmother sat trembling as she clutched the letter to her chest. Lillian wrapped a blanket around her sister, poured tea, and sat down beside her.

"Now, open it, Rhoda," she said. My grandmother was thirty-nine, just beginning to gray a little bit around the temples. She had not seen or heard from her surviving children in seven years, since that terrible Christmas when she tried to bring gifts. My grandfather aimed a shotgun at her head and told her never to come back.

"I can't. I just can't. You read it," she implored her sister. At this point I had placed the ring on my finger as I listened breathlessly. Gramma Rhoda got up from the table and went to her Empire chest, opened the top drawer, brought the letter to the kitchen, and placed it in front of me. She nodded that I should read it. I read:

January 3, 1933
Dearest Lost Mother,

Please forgive me, as I know I must forgive you. I do not know you except for what I can remember. I am sixteen now, and I think I know that I was told lies about you. I remember the fighting between you and Dad, but I also remember a good, kind mother. My brother is eighteen, and he joined the army. He is okay now, but I am in trouble.

Evelyn left Dad three years ago, and we moved in with Gramma. It was very crowded in her small house, but it was okay at first. Dad got odd jobs, and I tried to help, but Dad got sick, very sick. He is blind in one eye now, and the other eye is in danger. The doctor said it could be saved, but he needs medicine.

Mother, we have no money, we have no heat, and almost no food. I don't even have a winter coat. I don't know what to do. Can you help us please? I hope you still love me.
Your daughter,
Bunnie

I put the letter down, looked up at my grandmother, and asked, "My God, what did you do?" I already knew, because my mother had told the story many times, but I wanted to hear my grandmother's version. Rhoda, Lillian, and the boys pooled all their savings. Grandma bought a nice warm coat that she hoped would fit her daughter. They packed up as much food and wood as they could spare and extra blankets. My grandfather got his medicine; he and his mother had enough food and fuel until he recovered, and my mother became one more member around my aunt's long dinner table. My mother has often said that her mother turned out to be her best friend for the rest of her life.

"I know she says that," my grandmother pined, "but in my heart, I'm not sure she has ever forgiven me. How could she?" At thirteen I was totally puzzled about marital problems, and because my parents stayed together, I did not know anything at the time about having to choose sides as my mother did. I did not understand social and marital mores of the thirties, forties, and fifties. All of this I would study in a few years as a student in college, the first female in my family to do so, and a liberated woman of the sixties. Meanwhile, it made me sad to think that there was this wall between my mother and her mother, about which no one ever spoke.

"Grandma," I said, "I can see why you think the ring is magical. It's wonderful how your wish came true that Christmas season."

"You could call it a miracle," she replied. We sat silent for a while, listening to each other sip tea. Finally she stared directly into my eyes and said, "There's more you know, much more."

"What do you mean?"

"I used the ring one Christmas to bring your uncle home from the war."

She explained how she had had a hysterectomy and contacted a severe infection after the surgery. She did not ask for herself. All she asked for was to see her son one more time. He was with the 111st at Bastogne, and she was convinced he would have perished had he not been given compassionate leave to be beside her death-bed. He did not die, and neither did she.

"Around Christmas time in nineteen forty-nine, you were a very sick baby. You had spinal meningitis, and no one expected you to live. Your mother was instructed by your doctors to make your funeral preparations. I put the ring on, turned the stone toward my palm, held my hand to my heart, closed my eyes, and prayed for you. And here you are!" By now my grandmother had me absolutely intrigued. I think my jaw must have hung open.

"Oh, my darling, I could tell you so many more stories, and I will, but for now, I want you to know that the ring is yours. It's not your mother's, because she hasn't completely forgiven me, but it's yours because you have no reason to have to forgive me. Just know that it is magical. It's a ring of miraculous love. I do not know where or who it came from. I do not ask those questions. I only know that it works best during the holy season. It only works if the wish is given in selfless love, and you have to hold it to your heart and say, 'God, I give it all to You'." She stared at me with such intensity that after all these years, I can still see her face in that moment.

Of course, I followed her instructions. I kept it in a red sack and tucked it away secretly in a special drawer that I had. For years I only brought it out at Christmastime. I always told my grandmother what I was going to use it for and sought her approval, which she always gave.

I used it to bring my beloved cousin back from the Vietnam War, much as my grandmother had saved her son. I used it one year, 1967, during the Civil Rights movement to protect a black girl I met at college who reminded me of Sally Mae. We became fast friends because we shared the same name. Bernice insisted on following Father Groppi to participate in demonstrations in Milwaukee during that winter. He was a prime target, and she was in great danger. I used it to save my brother's leg after a surgery that went wrong. I used it to save a precious pet. I used it to hold onto my career as a teacher. I used it to help my father pass peacefully into the next world as he lay dying of cancer. He had the opportunity to say good-bye to everyone he loved and who loved him. All grievances were forgiven, and his final words were, "Don't worry, I am not afraid." But most importantly, I used it to bridge the great divide between my mother and my grandmother.

In the 1980s, before cell phones, Citizen Band radios were very popular. I had one, and it took me a year to learn the slang. I always signed out with "eighty-eights," which meant "love and kisses." Every time I said it, it made me remember my grandmother, who at eighty-eight, signed out with love and kisses. At her age, she had no business still renting out rooms to people living on the edge of life. But Rhoda was still sharp, strong, stubborn, and my mother and I loved her so much, we helped out on weekends. Mom and I did all the cleaning, mopping, and rent collecting, however sporadic. By this time, Gramma's beautiful house had slipped into definite slums, and many of her tenants tried to take advantage of her. My mother worried terribly and so wanted Gramma to try to sell the house and come live with her. As I said, Rhoda was stubborn. When the work was done, we three women would sit at the old Formica table with the chairs that didn't match to have a cup of celebratory "tay." Gramma always made it for us, but occasionally she would forget to put the tea bag in the water.

I was graduated from college and working at my first teaching position when it happened. Both my mother and my grandmother were extremely proud of me, a feeling I enjoyed very much because it bonded us when I often felt somehow in the middle between them.

If it had to happen, I was grateful that it happened just before my Christmas break from school. She should never have been on the third floor, but one of her tenants had left her a note that he was going out of town and would leave the rent money in an envelope under the mantel clock in his room. It was Advent, and Gramma wanted to buy presents for the family. It took her a good half hour to get up the staircases. She chose to go up the beautiful main staircase because she wanted to check in on her tenants and wish them happy holidays. James and Peter, two young Mormon men who were doing their ministry that year, were home at the time. So was Margarita, a young Hispanic woman who worked the night shift as a nurse's aid at St. Joseph's hospital. She was sleeping, but James and Peter had their door open a crack and returned my grandmother's greeting as she passed their door.

She collected the rent and decided to go down the servant's staircase, which led directly to the kitchen. She was tired and wanted a cup of tea, but she missed a step and tumbled down an entire flight of stairs. James and Peter heard her screams, and Margarita called the ambulance and my mother, who called me just as school was dismissing for the holidays.

I can no longer recall the details of talks with doctors or trying to piece together what had happened. I only remember that my grandmother was so broken that nothing could put her back together again. It was a marvel to everyone that she survived at all, but in a matter of hours, it became apparent that my grandmother had little time to live. Friends and family stopped in throughout the day. Even though she was heavily sedated on morphine, she recognized and greeted everyone. She ate nothing but accepted water. My mother and I decided to stay with her through the night. We asked for pillows and blankets and settled into the two large, stuffed chairs that were in the room.

We all dozed off, but I had a dream, and at two twenty-five in the morning, I woke my mother and told her I had to leave, but I'd be right back. She was very confused but too tired to resist. It seemed that I was instantly home. I flew to the drawer that held the tiny red sack. I took out the ring and put it on my finger, turning the stone to my palm. I immediately felt the heat. I placed my hand over my heart, closed my eyes, and said, "God, I give it all to you." Then I rushed back to the hospital.

I found my mother and grandmother holding hands, both in tears. My grandmother's breathing was very labored as she gestured to me to come close. I grabbed hold of her other hand and placed my ear next to her lips. She whispered, "She has forgiven me, my baby has forgiven me. Tell her about the ring." That was it, and I knew that the ring had worked another miracle, the most important miracle in my grandmother's life.

We buried Rhoda Elizabeth Merrill Scharoun two days later, in a style most befitting such a lady. Mom and I were overwhelmed by the many people who came to wish her farewell, friends and family yes, but also dozens of former tenants from throughout the years who had remembered her kindness in their time of need, people who had recovered from life's blows because they had at least a temporary safe haven in my grandmother's mansion.

After the service at the gravesite, as we walked back to the car, my mother said to me, "As painful as my own suffering was, I came to understand that my mother suffered more for my sake. Because I am a mother now, I understand that. You will be a mother someday, and you will understand." All I wanted was that my mother and grandmother could love and finally forgive each other. The Christmas ring made that happen.

We held onto the old house for a few months until it was purchased and demolished for the urban development projects of President Johnson's War on Poverty. We managed to salvage the beveled glass windows and the abstract florals, which have moved with us from house to house, but we could not save the great window. My grandmother's mansion became a daycare center for the impoverished children of the neighborhood. Mom said she was sure that grandma would be pleased.

My own daughter with the beautiful second soprano voice will soon be sixteen. She doesn't know *all* the lyrics yet, but I will teach her, and if she sings them well, I will give her the ring this coming Christmas season.

"ASK NOT FOR WHOM THE BELL TOLLS"

The announcement came upon us like a thundercloud, a tornado, a tsunami; the point is, no one believed, no one wanted to believe that such a thing could happen. Everyone prayed that it never would. The community was shocked and overwhelmed.

Personally, I did not know the man, never met him, but I had a sense of him because I overheard bits and pieces of his sister's conversations in the lunchroom at the school where we both work. In spite of her sometimes typical sisterly complaints, it was clear that she and her twin sister loved him deeply, that he was an important part and influence in their lives, and that they admired him. Nevertheless, I felt a piece of myself torn, and I wept.

It has been over thirty years now since I felt this kind of loss, since I served with the American Red Cross in Vietnam. I was very young then, twenty-two, but in a year's time, I aged rapidly. Then, on a daily basis, I was confronted with the loss of great potential. I was forced to wonder what these young individuals might have experienced in their lives, what they might have contributed to the world had they lived. I remembered the grief of those who loved, admired, and believed in them, who had laughed and cried with them, how I tried to comfort the survivors while suffering myself, wondering why this hurt so damned bad. Would I ever get used to this, or at least enough to get through the year? I now know what a stupid thought that was. There is no limit to pain, no end. What hurts in a moment hurts forever; it just gets muted so that we who have to remain behind can deal with it. We suppress it in order to get on with our lives, but every now and then…we remember.

My husband, who did not even know my friend, the sister, wept for the loss of this young man's life. He should be so hard, a soldier, a veteran, a member of the

CIA, someone who knows about the death and dying of young people for whatever cause might seem right at the time, who doesn't want to speak about some of his experiences, for good reason. My husband, like me, was one of many people drawn to the chapel to take the time to celebrate one man's life, a man we didn't even know.

The chapel was full of people on this Saturday morning, a time in modern America that most people sleep in to rest from the week or race around maniacally to get errands done, but this man's passing made so very many stop for two hours to think, hungry to think about life and what it means and why we live it, because they all have their own stories. What bound us consciously or unconsciously to come together on that sunny Saturday morning to weep the loss of life and celebrate the life of this one man?

Music—he was a man of music, and music is magic. I think music must be the way God speaks to us and may be the best way that we get to speak to God. It is his music that brought us all, however diverse, together in our desire that morning to celebrate his life.

As we gathered and waited for the priest to speak, the beautiful chapel, a focal point of the university, was filled with the music of a guitarist and choral voices. The notes floated around the chapel, softly bouncing off the marble pillars like ethereal bubbles glistening in the soft light. It wasn't at all sad music, rather it was uplifting, full of hope, and as I glanced around the pews, I saw faint smiles on people's faces, some with dreamy looks in their eyes, others with their eyes closed.

Both sisters struggled to give their eulogies, their shock and grief weighing so heavily upon them, yet they just had to declare their special love before a community that loved them, as well as their brother. The women began to weep, and the handkerchiefs appeared from gentle, sympathetic hands. The music stopped for the moment, and the priest began. He spoke of many things about this young man who left us all so soon, yet each thing was tied to and filled with music. He painted a picture that each of us could visualize in our own way of this man getting lost in the music during rehearsals, how he would improvise and make the music his own. It was his particular gift to the world, his soul's speech, God's voice coming through him. Now the men were openly weeping, including my husband. Before the end of the service, the family gave the congregation a CD called *Passion,* which was filled with their son's, their brother's, musical contribution.

My husband and I did not fulfill our plans, our chores, for that day. Instead, we went home and changed with hardly a word between us, except the perfunctory ones. We went for a long ride in the country and stopped in the park. We so needed to feel the air, smell the grass, touch the trees, and see people involved in nature, at one with God. We needed to process what we had experienced that morning.

I came very close to dying three times in my life. I have no fear of it. Listening to the CD took me back through each experience. The music felt like a hand holding mine and "leading me through green pastures." All three times, there were green, green, green pastures just beyond the disease, the water, and the fire. And beyond the green, the wonders and the joy are impossible to describe, but there is always a choice. I knew each time that I could cross the Rainbow Bridge; I felt such an overwhelming sense of coming home, and I was given the choice. But *my* work was not done. I had a great deal more to do, not the least of which was to give birth to two more music makers.

BIOGRAPHY

Born in Syracuse, New York to second-generation immigrant parents, Bobbie Trotter is the second female in the extended family to achieve a college education. She majored in English and began teaching high school in the late 1960s. She still teaches full time at Mount Saint Joseph Academy for young women in Flourtown, Pennsylvania, and part time for Gwynedd Mercy College in East Norriton, Pennsylvania.

Much affected by the sacrifice of friends and family in the Vietnam War, she temporarily left teaching and volunteered with the American Red Cross to serve in the Republic of South Vietnam from 1970-1971 as a "Donut Dollie." Years later, she became active in the Vietnam Women's Memorial Project and ultimately donated eight of her poems to *Visions of War, Dreams of Peace*, an anthology of poetry written by women who served in Vietnam. The proceeds went to the women's project to help pay for the statue, which now stands in Washington, D.C. Bobbie was selected to read two of her poems at the candlelight dedication in 1993.

Her experience in Vietnam gave her a great appreciation for America's military. In 1975 she joined the Air National Guard and served for thirty years, finally retiring as a Chief Master Sergeant.

She has two grown children, a son, Ross, and a daughter, Megan, of whom she is very proud. She lives in Norristown, Pennsylvania, with her husband, Jack, and their terrier, Lilly.